IS IT JUST ME OR IS EVERYONE FAMOUS?

IS IT JUST ME OR IS EVERYONE FAMOUS?

FROM A-LIST TO Z LIST AND HOW TO MAKE IT YOURSELF

TONY COWELL

JOHN BLAKE

Published by John Blake Publishing Ltd,
3 Bramber Court, 2 Bramber Road,
London W14 9PB, England

www.blake.co.uk

First published in paperback in 2007

ISBN 978 1 84454 316 8

British Library Cataloguing-in-Publication Data:

A catalogue record for this book is available from the British Library.

Design by www.envydesign.co.uk

Printed and bound in Great Britain by Creative Print and Design,
Ebbw Vale, Wales

1 3 5 7 9 10 8 6 4 2

Papers used by John Blake Publishing are natural, recyclable
products made from wood grown in sustainable forests.
The manufacturing processes conform to the environmental regulations
of the country of origin.

Every attempt has been made to contact the relevant copyright-holders,
but some were unobtainable. We would be grateful if the appropriate
people could contact us.

To my mother Julie

Photographs © WENN/Nikki Nelson /*New York Daily News*/CAPITOL/Adriana M Barraza/Z Tomaszewski/Dan Wooller/David Livingston/Vince Maher/PNP/Daniel Deme/Adriana M Barraza/Spirit Pictures/Carrie Devorah /Emma Bryant /L Gallo/Tina Paul /Simon Burchell/David Mepham/Dimitri Halkidis/POP/Charlie Ottley/Michel Utrecht/Spirit Pictures/James Coldrey/Harsha Gopal.

Foreword

Once upon a time there was only one television station and there was only one radio station, and the television was only on for a few hours a day, so the number of famous people around was tiny. Yeah, you're right – it was a good time to live! Now there are hundreds of TV stations and thousands of radio stations as well as the Internet, so the chances to become famous have multiplied enormously.

Ever since we started the first series of *Pop Idol*, a door has been open for hundreds of people to get their 15 minutes of fame. But 15 minutes of fame does not a famous person make! Just because you dress up as a banana doesn't mean that you'l be remembered as a great singer. People might remember the banana, but not the person inside the skin. (Thank God!)

To be truly famous and not just a one-night blur, you need talent, modesty and belief. The Cowell family know all about fame. Simon is now one big famous person – worldwide. But he is also one of those rare people who understand how the fame game works, and he doesn't pull punches. You know why? Because he knows what fame means. Every person he listens to in auditions he feels for. He knows what its like to be a wannabe. He was once a wannabe. I was a wannabe.

In the 1980s when I had just about every top recording artist (and wannabe) pop singer knocking on my studio door I had to make that same decision (as Simon, Louis and Sharon do today on *The X Factor*) – yes or no? Do you, or do you not have what it takes? At that point you are dealing with peoples' hopes and dreams. It's a tough old business – and suddenly their life is in your hands.

Can you imagine what it felt like for the actors that were called up to audition to be the new James Bond? That was one giant, life-changing monster of a part up for grabs – and only one person can get it. The fame game is bloody cruel, but if you want to be famous you have to be able to handle rejection – even on this massive scale. Can you imagine what it feels likes to be the actor that lost out to Daniel Craig? What does he tell his wife and kids – 'I was nearly the next James Bond'?

Talent is one of those commodities which everyone believes they have but is in fact a rarity. Modesty is a defining feature of most famous people. Conversely, there is a dearth of it in people who lack talent. To have belief is good, but blind faith takes you to another place.

Remember the banana? Well, to stay on top means that you don't have to dress up as one, but if you were a banana that could sing – then that would be amazing!

To be famous takes only a moment, to be famously remembered takes a lifetime, and this fantastic book will show you how!

Pete Waterman

Acknowledgements

No book would be complete without thanking those who helped make it happen. So thank you to all everyone who played a huge part in its preparation, notably Pete Waterman, who despite what my brother thinks, should be back on TV where he belongs.

Thanks to my editor Clive Hebard, to Katie Price, Shane Lynch and Mark Frith, editor of *Heat* magazine.

Thanks to everyone at:

beonscreen.com, wisdomquotes.com,

forbes.com and realityTVmagazine.com.

Thanks to Helen at PWL, to the *Sun* newspaper, all at Channel 4, ITV's *This Morning*, and to Michael Barrymore, for helping me choose the best book to write.

Thanks to Nick, Kane, Dor Dor and Harrison for

making me happy and letting me stay in their shed. Finally, thanks to Emma Jo, for her love, support and creative contributions to the book. And of course my little (but now chubby) brother Simon, who continues to inspire me.

Contents

Introduction

Fame: the final frontier...

My postman met his wife on *Blind Date*. My next-door neighbour appeared on *Wife Swap*. The man who runs the corner shop was Paul Anka on *Stars in Your Eyes* and my nephew is about to go on *The X Factor*.

If there is one thing reality television has taught the masses it's that everybody wants to be famous. A recent survey of twelve-year-old schoolchildren showed that 72 per cent of them want to be on television when they grow up. When I was at school everyone wanted to be a train driver, a doctor, or a nurse – reality TV is alive and well.

The quest for fame is now a booming industry. Websites like Springboard UK list every reality TV show looking for contestants. Audition for a pop band; apply for voiceover work; try your hand at songwriting or get an acting job – the world is your oyster! If you want to pose for a lad's mag, just send in your saucy photo. And guess what? No experience is required! Call me a cynic, but I can't help thinking that it may be a tad easier for girls to get onboard the fame train. Agencies that specialise in work for nannies, PAs or assistants to celebrities are now big business. Advertisements that claim, 'Celebrity assistants get to experience the lives of the rich and famous' may well entice the civilians of the world to have their fifteen minutes of fame with the stars of their choice, then sell the intimate secrets for some quick cash to establish themselves in the pages of *Heat*.

Celebrity gossip is a huge tabloid business. There have been a few notable successes including the stories from Paul Burrell, Rebecca Loos and Faria Alam. Although, it's fair to say that only Paul Burrell has achieved fame, and long-term financial rewards from capitalising on his job with the Princess of Wales.

By wangling a job working for a celeb or a royal you will always be on top of the hottest trends in style, fashion, art and design, and will often be given a stack of cash to go out and buy things for your celebrity. In fact, many celebrity PAs receive new furniture, jewellery or other expensive gifts from their celeb employees. American TV star Carol Burnett gave her assistant a Land Rover. Wow! There is also the very strong chance you will become close and intimate with your celebrity. They may take you in as their confidante, since they know they can trust you with their most personal secrets. Yeah right.

Iwannabefamous.com has to be the most hilarious website. Claiming, 'We are looking for someone just like you! We feature one person per day and make them famous [sic] by featuring them on our website. Because of all the publicity this site has received lately, being featured on our website really can make you famous!' Really – how?

Let us cut to the chase. If you want to be famous, you do it yourself. Don't frig about with the Internet. If you really want to be famous you will be, but first you must be addicted to celebrity.

OK, you're busted! You are officially diagnosed with CELEBRITY ADDICTION. There are five main characteristics of this disease:

1. You have an insatiable desire to find out what celebrities are doing and what they said to whom and where they said it.
2. You try to copy hairstyles and fashion of the stars.
3. You purchase and subscribe to all the magazines that have celebrity coverage.
4. You record all of the television shows that have celebrity coverage.
5. You can't believe it when your favourite celebrity does something human – like have a bad hair day or get mad at someone.

It is safe to say that the majority of people in the Britain have celebrity addiction. Otherwise, how do all the magazines, newspapers and TV shows survive? Even though celebrities are well paid nowadays, it must be very hard to be under such constant scrutiny on a day-to-day basis. This, if you succeed will be your greatest test.

Celebrity addiction has many of us star struck, but it is no longer enough to bask in the glory of other people's fame. Now everyone wants a go at being famous. The Beckhams, Jordan, Jade Goody, Brad Pitt and Angelina help sell millions of magazines – we cannot get enough of them. Celebrity gossip has become like the blob in that Steve McQueen movie: it spreads everywhere it can.

Tony Cowell – March 2007

UNDER-TENS SAY BEING A CELEBRITY IS THE WORLD'S 'BEST THING'
As we went to press, a poll of 1,500 under-tens revealed that being a celebrity is 'the best thing in the world'. God was ranked as their tenth favourite thing, with celebrity, good looks and being rich at one, two and three!

1
The History of Fame

 The golden age of Hollywood and the birth of the gossip magazine gave us the first celebs. In those heady days, they were inspirational and untouchable – and they had class. From Charlie Chaplin, Mary Pickford, Rudolph Valentino through to Clark Gable, Ava Gardner, Joan Crawford and Grace Kelly, the public adored their idols and the luxury and glamour afforded by their careers. In 1946, the average earnings for these stars were between $150,000–$200,000 per film. Mr Cruise, please take note.

The birth of television in the 1950s created a new demand for an ever-increasing number of 'stars'. Reality television is the logical extreme of this and, coupled with the tabloid newspapers' hunger for celebrity gossip, you now have a whole new generation of celebrities. Suddenly, film stars could boost their earnings by getting on TV.

So how much do we really need to know about our idols, screen gods and goddesses? Didn't curiosity kill the cat? Clearly not, as the hunger for celebrity gossip has never been more voracious. We want to know everything about our celebs – good or bad – and preferably bad.

How could Clarke Gable ever have lived up to every woman's expectations, and yet, in the minds of his fans, he did; and how very devastating to discover now that he suffered from severe halitosis! *Gone with the Wind* will never be the same.

We dissect them, pull apart their sense of style, their partner choices, their core beliefs… wouldn't it be better if we knew nothing at all and just viewed them as mysterious, enigmatic objects of beauty?

Judy Garland is now looked upon as a tragic figure, who was addicted to uppers, downers and weight controllers by the time she reached puberty. She married a man who turned out to be gay, and then married another who beat her and took all her money. I think we should remember her as the spunky girl next door who followed the yellow brick road and wore shoes that every little girl covets.

During their time, the so-called Golden Age of Hollywood actors were glamorous and fabulous. Nobody wanted to see them fall on their faces. We wanted them to have the beautiful other half, keep their gay affairs to themselves and bonk animals, vegetables and minerals in the privacy of their own homes without the threat of kiss and tell. The public were more interested then in having their escapist fantasies fulfilled, and were apparently less concerned about bringing their idols down to a more mundane level. The sordid, depraved and trivial aspects of their heroes' personal lives were pretty much left undisturbed, leaking out over the course of time to raised eyebrows and gasps of astonishment, but not much more. Reputations and golden images remained virtually intact.

The celebrities were chosen and they were special. Marilyn Monroe is one of the most under-rated actresses Hollywood has ever produced. Nowadays, she is remembered as the blonde bombshell who bedded a president and was bumped off by the Secret Services because of their entanglement... she is rarely remembered as the gorgeous, comic genius of *Gentlemen Prefer Blondes* and *Some Like It Hot*, and the inspiration for hundreds of starlets that

3

followed, including Madonna, Christina Aguilera and Scarlett Johansson.

The Queen of Pop is a classic case of TMI – too much information. Her Royal Madgeness is the queen of image reinvention; few people haven't seen her perform an act of oral sex on a bottle of water, expose her cervix in her coffee-table book *Sex* or simulate sex with 'Jesus' in a video. Information overload! She's served herself up on a plate, and thrust virtually every aspect of her life and fantasies down the public's throat for years. Enough! If ever there was a case for asking someone to leave something to the imagination, then Madonna is it – our imaginations are under-used enough as it is.

For a celebrity in the time BC – Before Clifford – you relied on the studios to cover up your discrepancies, fix your nose, wire your jaw, satiate your every perverse demand and trusted that nobody would ever find out. It was in the studio's interest to cover up their most bankable stars' misdemeanours. Celebs would often retreat from public life, and hide out in a secret sanctuary until the scandal had passed or the rumour mill had moved on.

However, as the public's appetite for gossip increased, the studios' effectiveness in covering their tracks started to falter, especially when their stars committed crimes. For many years, Hollywood concealed secrets, although most of us now know that Judy Garland was a drug addict; Marilyn underwent several cosmetic procedures, and had an equally creative love life; Rock Hudson was gay; and that the then married Clark Gable had a child with Oscar-winner Loretta Young.

The heads of the studios were the original spin-doctors and controlled almost every aspect of the actor's life. Mayer of MGM was apparently homophobic, and expected his matinée idols to be butch 'he-men' and appeal strictly to the female movie-going public. Mayer, being a control freak, knew that some of his stars would frequent whore houses, so to protect them from disease and from one night-stand pregnancies, he set one up himself.

Everyone has been at it since time began – the difference is that we now have an unquenchable thirst for gossip, and an ever-growing, multi-million-pound market that fuels the tittle-tattle through television, magazines, the tabloids, the Internet…everyone has access to it, and it's instantly available.

During the Golden Age of Hollywood, the public had very different ideas of what was moral and decent. In 1934, the industry had to react to a public outcry over sultry sex siren Mae West's on- and off-screen antics. The Hays Code was implemented and offered guidelines for the industry, stating that:

1. No picture shall be produced that will lower the moral standards of those who see it. Hence the sympathy of the audience should never be thrown to the side of crime, wrongdoing, evil or sin.

2. Correct standards of life, subject only to the requirements of drama and entertainment, shall be presented.

The code remained in place until the 1960s, after which the public appeared more tolerant of what was shown on screen and, therefore, what subsequently went on off screen – and as their tolerance was raised, so was their curiosity. The personal lives of the highest-profile stars had become just as marketable as the films they appeared in, and the public appetite for peeking behind the scenes, and uncovering real people with flaws and deficiencies, just like them, became an industry in its own right.

2
Hollywood Scandal –
The Golden Age

ERROL FLYNN

Errol's life seemed to be one big scandal, but the real humdinger came in 1943 when he went on trial, accused of having had illegal sex with a teen on his yacht – he was acquitted.

Life was wild for the man fondly remembered for donning tights and springing about in Sherwood Forest; one of his drinking buddies once stole the dead body of his actor friend John Barrymore and popped it in a chair at Flynn's home. If walls could talk, then that house could fill the pages of any tabloid! There were many wild parties, and it was said that Flynn had two-way mirrors installed so he could watch his guests perform.

HEDY LAMARR

The *Samson and Delilah* actress was accused of shoplifting in 1966 at the May & Co department store in LA. A jury found her not guilty and she sued the store for $5 million.

It has also been alleged that she indulged in orgies and enjoyed relations with other women.

JOAN CRAWFORD

According to her daughter, Christina, in her best-selling book *Mommie Dearest*, the star of *Whatever Happened to Baby Jane?* had physically and emotionally abused her.

Her sexuality has also been the subject of endless speculation.

ROCK HUDSON

Rock Hudson knew how the system worked, and he needed the system to work for him. Many of the

leading journalists at the time knew that Hudson was gay, but betraying that confidence would be 'bad for business', so it remained hush-hush.

Hudson was always pictured with a new, gorgeous female 'companion' in public and, in 1955, he married Phyllis Gates, his agent's secretary. They divorced three years later. Following his death in 1986 from AIDS, the world came to terms with the shocking revelation that the pretty-boy pin-up had been gay. He was the first major star to die of the modern plague and it appeared that he had led an alternative private life to the one the studios had led us all to believe.

CLARKE GABLE

Despite suffering from halitosis, Gable had apparently enjoyed a great deal of success in the bedroom – allegedly with both sexes. It's also said that Gable had a fling with fellow actor Billy Haines. He also fathered Loretta Young's child when he was married, forcing Young to 'adopt' her own child to avoid scandal.

MARILYN MONROE

Hollywood's most fleshy commodity and the ultimate blonde bombshell was the first nude cover girl of *Playboy*.

Some have described her as a nymphomaniac, and there is no denying that she had a healthy sex life. She dated actors, singers, politicians and their brothers… she wasted no time in sampling as much as possible from her own particular candy store! There have been rumours of three-in-a-bed romps, orgies,

abortions and, of course, her addiction to drink and drugs. As her substance abuse worsened in the latter stages of her career, more stories of on-set tantrums, absences, memory loss and poor performances began to leak out in the press. The fact is, Marilyn just needed love and affection and, despite all the scandal surrounding her, the public still adores her.

LANA TURNER

It's alleged that Turner and Mickey Rooney had an affair in the late 1930s, which resulted in an abortion. Turner denied the rumour. She was married seven times, but yearned for the love of Tyrone Power, who was in love with Judy Garland. Turner is also said to have had a liaison with Clarke Gable, but she insisted that they had shared no off-screen chemistry.

FRANK SINATRA

As the Mafia's favourite singer, Sinatra never shunned press attention, but lived his life in the full glare of the paparazzi. He appeared to be the epitome of Hollywood glamour.

Throughout his career, Sinatra had a highly ambivalent relationship with fame. The singer lived and gloried in that public gaze, and liked to eat in restaurants and drink in bars, rather than shutting himself away in seclusion. He married his childhood sweetheart, Nancy Barbato, in 1939 and had three children.

However, just ten years later, his affair with Ava Gardner became a massive public scandal, he was fired from his radio show, dropped by MGM and was released from contract by his agent. It turned out to be a very bad year.

When it came to women, Sinatra even tested the wares before recommending them to the president JFK. In 1975, when Jacqueline Kennedy Onassis slept with Sinatra, she allegedly discovered that the singer had arranged mistresses for her husband, and so, to avoid scandal, never saw him again. Sinatra was devastated.

MAKE OR BREAK?

What is particularly interesting now is to examine how the power of a scandal has shifted. Before the 1970s, it could potentially destroy the career of a star with just one tabloid revelation. How unlike today, when you consider such  scandals as 'Cocaine Kate Moss', whose earnings have at least doubled since she was pictured having a good old snort; and Pete Doherty is another whose popularity continues to grow as public interest in the troubled Babyshambles lead singer never wanes, despite his constant run-ins with the police.

But the universal thread remains – the power of the press. It is true that it can make or break you. Will there ever be a story in the papers about Michael Jackson without a mention of the child molestation charges of which he was acquitted? Or one about Michael Barrymore that ignores the party at which Stuart Lubbock was found floating in the swimming pool? There is no escape from the prying eyes of the paparazzi and the tittle-tattle of the tabloids.

TODAY'S GOSSIPMONGERS

There are more newspapers and magazines now than ever. The weekly glossies, the monthlies – they all have their available column inches for wannabe celebs. The opportunities nowadays for exposés, scandals and exclusive disclosures are almost endless, but the public's interest does not stop there. When real scandals are hard to come by – and let's face it, film stars are rarely caught sleeping with presidents or prime ministers these days – the press has to make do with a slightly less earth-shattering type of gossip. Acres of pages in papers and magazines are filled with celebrity sightings, pictures of singers picking their noses, soap stars out shopping or picking their children up from school, reality TV stars falling out of bars and clubs, and actors sitting in restaurants with mystery blondes. It may not make the front pages, but the public still wants its fix, and anything that relates to celebrity is fair game. The flipside of that coin is obviously that the celebrities themselves have got much smarter about playing the press and keeping themselves in the public eye.

Perhaps Princess Diana was the quintessential, modern-day example of this phenomenon – on the one hand, damning the press for intrusion, and the paparazzi for snapping her every move, while on the other, forging alleged secret deals with editors and photographers to maintain her image and profile in the press, and leaking juicy titbits of information that would keep a gossip-hungry public interested, sympathetic… and eager for more.

So, if you want to be famous, you need to be prepared to act fast and milk that mother for all it is worth. Edit and censor your life; be prepared to talk about anything and everything; and bare your soul to whoever will listen.

The shelf life of a star is shorter than it used to be. It is cut-throat, swift and highly disposable, so much so that the fame of a *Big Brother* contestant rarely lasts long enough to overlap the following series. You may get your 15 minutes, or you may only get 5 – you probably won't get your chance again, so give people something to sink their teeth into.

3
All About Celebrity

'We live in a fame epidemic – it's like a disease.'
SIMON COWELL

Celebrity is the defining issue of the 21st century. In recent years, much has been made and written of the rise of contemporary celebrity culture. Writers, thinkers and pundits alike warn us of the danger of our obsession with celebrity, even as more and more of us tune into TV gossip and buy magazines like *OK*, *Now* and *Heat*. Andy Warhol's cynical prediction that everyone will be famous for 15 minutes has virtually become a national rallying cry as television offers seemingly unlimited opportunities to enable anyone and everyone to appear in the spotlight – *Big Brother*, *The X Factor*, *How Do You Solve a Problem Like Maria?*, *Trisha*, *Ant and Dec's Saturday Night Takeaway*… the list of potential fame-making shows has grown out of all proportion, and the public's appetite for such programming has developed accordingly. And the format of the shows, in which you can go immediately from zero to hero, has had to keep pace with this growth. It's no longer sufficient to thrust some wannabe pop star in the limelight with microphone and a couple of backing singers. Been there, done it, got the T-shirt. Nowadays, the more outrageous and attention grabbing the format, the better.

The more that is written about fame, the less shocked we become. That's the way things are, so why not grab your moment in the *Sun*? Popularity, celebrity's essential fuel, is a standard part of the human psyche, along with envy and desire. In the distant past, gods and demons (and gladiators) were the superstars, and everything that had significant impact on people – positive or negative – was attributed to them. Modern storytelling has its roots in gossip. Royalty always made everyone's A-list, or at least we were led to believe so, just in case they felt the need to raise their profile with some attention-grabbing beheadings and impalings. Mass entertainment has been with us all along too, with an ever-widening definition of 'mass', which has created a whole new species – if you are neither god nor royal, then you must be a celebrity.

But how long will you last? Who will remember you next week, month... decade? No matter how much good Bob Geldof or Bono do to address world poverty, and make a real difference to millions of people's lives, they are likely to be forgotten – history has a habit of glossing over the exploits of the good, in favour of the perennial attraction of the truly evil. And if you don't believe me, think back over the entire span of human history, and name ten mass murderers or despotic world leaders... and now name ten Nobel prize winners. Somehow, the bad guys always seem to make so much more of an impact.

For Brad, Angelina and all the others craving the public's long-term attention, the lesson is that real longevity – in which people will still be mentioning your name two centuries from now – requires truly outrageous behaviour, and scandal on a massive scale, sufficient to attract the vultures and give them enough meat to pick over for years to come.

In America, Philadelphians celebrated the 200th birthday of Shakespearian actor Edwin Forrest, whom the *Los Angeles Times* referred to as 'the original star'. He was so popular in his day, his crazed fans caused a riot in New York that killed more than 20 people. The actor's 1851 divorce trial drew the equivalent of today's 24-hour cable coverage; the transcripts sold in two volumes. Why was Forrest so popular? Why is anyone?

WHAT IS A CELEBRITY?

Modern-day celebrities are hard to avoid, and the stars of today are a far cry from their ancient counterparts. Newspapers boost sales by splashing stars across their front pages, and magazines are bursting with them, from the A-list – David Beckham, Julia Roberts –down to, well, the murkiest scrapings at the bottom of a very dodgy barrel. They know who they are, and if you're not sure, then take yourself off to your local nightclub on a Thursday night. If they've got a 'celebrity' guest to turn up and 'dazzle' the punters, then that's the other end of the scale – Z-list, the 'celebrities' who have perhaps shone for a nanosecond on a TV soap, who did an advert for shampoo, or who came third on *Big Brother 2*, and are desperate to squeeze every last penny out of their moment in the spotlight, before sinking back again into obscurity and the thing that every celeb dreads the most – *not being recognised*.

Prime-time TV is also rife with stars clamouring to promote their latest venture, while millions of fans clog up cyberspace with websites paying homage to their heroes. The Internet has certainly helped fuel the celebrity fires.

But all of this is in stark contrast to some of the earliest records of celebrity, when getting noticed involved more than just wearing a skimpy dress to a film première. Thousands of years ago, one of the best ways to gain fame was through a title, such as 'monarch', or to be a warrior whose deeds had a direct impact on the lives of their fellow countrymen. But this was not the only way to grab the attention of the masses or have your name inscribed across the pages of the history books.

Some of the first celebrities were, in fact, winners in the ancient Olympic Games, and the first recorded Olympic champion was a naked runner, Coroebus, a cook from Elis, who won the sole event, the 'stade', at the Olympics in 776 BCE, which was a run of approximately 192 metres.

The famous religious books of the world's faiths are full of examples of individuals who are well known to the general public. Some of the pharaohs of ancient Egypt set in motion devices to ensure their own fame for centuries to come. The pyramids were a symbol of their importance and renown, and screamed, 'Don't you bloody forget that I once ruled here, and I was very rich and powerful, so remember that every time you look at this huge pointy monument that took thousands of people years to build. Aren't I great?'

As time moved on, celebrity culture was no longer restricted to royalty and biblical or mythical figures – it began to pervade every sector of society, including business, publishing and even academia.

Mass media has increased the exposure and power of celebrity. A trend has developed that celebrity carries with it increasingly more social capital than in earlier times. Each nation or cultural community – linguistic, ethnic or religious – has its own independent celebrity system, but this is becoming less the case due to globalisation.

So what is a celebrity? Before that now overused

term appeared, were people just 'renowned'… well known? They are no longer astral bodies out of our reach. In the 1920s, movie producers used to withhold the identities of their actors but public demand forced them to offer up some essential details – whether they had partners/mistresses,  how they lived, where they went. And so it began… We crave details about the ins and outs of perfect strangers' private lives. Is it necessary to know as much as possible? Too right it is!

The definition of 'celebrity' is someone who is famous during his or her lifetime and is well known for what they do; from the Latin *celebritas*; French *celeber*, meaning 'famous'. That definition, though, is no longer strictly true. People can achieve legendary status by dying young, but aren't they still a celebrity despite not being around us any longer? James Dean made three films, yet he has been hailed one of the greatest screen actors who ever lived, despite many being unable to name all three movies on his CV – *East of Eden, Rebel Without a Cause* and *Giant*.

Brat Pack actor River Phoenix became another 20th-century icon by dying young. If he were alive today and had checked in and out of the Betty Ford

Clinic, traipsed around with a tiny dog or embarrassed himself on national TV, wouldn't he be thought of as one of the leading celebrities of his generation?

Another factor nowadays is that you don't actually have to do anything to be famous. You don't need a particular talent – the royals have been doing it for years and it's finally caught on. Other privileged members of the upper classes can not only be found prowling around the trendiest clubs and bars, but also trying their manicured hands at reality TV and presenting. Lady Victoria Hervey, Paris Hilton, James Hewitt, Tara Palmer-Tomkinson... all are regularly in the press and have found a place in the public consciousness, famous merely for being famous.

Liz Hurley upstaged her boyfriend at his big film première and got her gorgeous, semi-naked body splashed all over the tabloids, to lasting positive effect on her profile and career.

One strange phenomenon is that while celebrity status is widely sought after, celebrities are often unhappy with that status. The modern curse of 'paparazzi' is a problem for celebrities, as well as celebrity marriages. Child celebrities are notorious for having poor emotional health in adulthood, and have been known to turn to drug or alcohol abuse when their celebrity fades.

A common complaint of modern celebrity culture is that the public, instead of appreciating virtues or talents in celebrities, are more interested in those who are the most willing to break ethical boundaries, or those who are most aggressive in self-promotion. In other words, infamy has replaced fame. The roles of the town drunk, the court jester or the sex kitten are not new, but arguably, the glorification of these individuals is. Pete Doherty is now more famous for his indiscretions than for any particular talent or skill, but he is no less adored by the media and public despite that.

One possible explanation for this trend is that an artificial need for celebrity has been created in order to promote a product or a service, rather than to allow the growth of a particular celebrity out of a purely biographical event. As more new products are launched in a world market that is constantly expanding, the need for more celebrities has become an industry in itself. Paris Hilton has become the ultimate 'It' girl and is now a global brand. It's only a matter of time before Pete Doherty will follow with his own brand of cologne and aftershave – although you will probably have to sniff it rather than spray it.

CELEBRITIES AND THE PAPARAZZI

They are the most creative, selfish, arrogant and ambitious breed of people ever to have walked the planet. Celebrities or the paparazzi? Both... one can't survive without the other; they both despise and need each other; they feed off one another; it's the perfect symbiotic relationship. To be successful at either career, you must be ruthless, relentless and utterly focused. It's

give and take, and if you can get away with a little give, and a whole lot more take, then you're on to a winner.

The word 'paparazzo' first appeared as the name of a character in Fellini's 1960 movie *La Dolce Vita*. He was a photographer who made his money snapping over-fed, decadent and glamorous victims, capturing their images and activities and selling them to the papers for personal gain. Fellini himself said of the character, 'Paparazzo suggests to me a buzzing insect, hovering, darting, stinging,' and he also drew an image of the character, that depicts a sort of vampirish insectile, implying that paparazzi, like mosquitoes, are also parasites.

But the birth of the celebrity snappers wasn't instantaneous. Sophia Loren was one of the first actresses to employ a photographer – it made sense. If pictures of you are going to be 'out there' anyway, it's advisable to retain as much control over them as possible, and it's far better that they're fabulous. We have evolved past that, much to our delight and the celebs' horror; we don't want 'fabulous' pictures any more – entire studios are set up to produce those – we want to see spots, wrinkles, fat, cellulite and underarm hair, and if we can get all of them in one picture, then that's fantastic!

Why do we all seem to hate the paparazzi? If it weren't for them, we wouldn't have our weekly fix from *Heat* magazine, and the pages of *Hello!*, *OK*, *Closer* and *Reveal* would be full of *writing*! Ugh! I don't want to have to *read* about semi-naked nymphettes, or royals wearing Nazi swastikas, or lead singers having a brawl outside a nightclub... I want to *see* them!

We, the public, are surely responsible for unleashing these monsters on poor, innocent, famous people? If you have never witnessed snappers in action, you would be shocked; they relentlessly pursue their target and drop them just as fast. And we're not talking about the relatively orderly row of snappers popping their flashbulbs on either side of a red carpet – the true paparazzi are those who tail the famous with the specific purpose of getting a shot of them doing something odd, depraved, sensational, illegal, or anything that goes against the image they may be trying to portray to the public. Those are the shots that make real money, sometimes hundreds of thousands of pounds. The paparazzi who hounded Princess Diana for years were well aware of the rewards, and did everything they could to get the picture that would make them a million. Memorable shots included Diana's 'cellulite' as she ran to her car; Diana's anguished face as she learnt of her father's death; Diana diving gracefully into the sea from the deck of Dodi's private yacht... our lives were undoubtedly enriched by having access to these images. Weren't they? In our society, it has become the only form of stalking that is still legal.

Charlotte Church seems to have a more modern approach to the burden of the paparazzi. She knows they'll be there, so why try to alter her life around them? She apparently doesn't give a stuff about the types of pictures they get of her – walking to the shops with fluffy slippers and a fag hanging out of her mouth; staggering out of a Cardiff nightclub in the small hours with a tank full of Bacardi Breezers – she fabulously ignores them and tells them they're bastards.

The Beckhams are the masters of out-manoeuvring the paps. The seemingly spontaneous shots of them shopping for jeans, or having a haircut, are carefully orchestrated by their people tipping off the snappers. The trouble is, it can all backfire. You use the media for your own gain, and you then become tabloid fodder. It's open season as far as the Beckhams are concerned, and whether they're in favour, in Marbella, incognito or in transit – we can't escape them.

Major broadcasting corporations have Beckham correspondents, people paid to tag the couple and keep abreast of their whereabouts and activities. They are on a par with the royals in terms of what they do and its editorial significance. It is remarkable if you stop and think about the rise and rise of the Beckhams, and their lifestyle now when compared to their roots – he is a shy, inarticulate footballer from Essex, and she is an ex-pop star who likes shopping. Who was it who said that the meek shall inherit the earth?

In August 1997, our view of the paparazzi changed for ever. They were blamed for the death of the 'people's princess', the mistress of paparazzi manipulation. Having chased and hounded her for years, Diana, Princess of Wales had died in a car crash in Paris, and the snappers were there to capture every single moment. Even when she was dead, she was still photo fodder. They had just lost the world's most photographed woman.

As has been mentioned already, Princess Diana played the paps almost to perfection at times. At first she feared them; their intrusion and demands on her were too much for the vulnerable young woman thrust into the limelight. She soon cottoned on, though, and began to use them to great effect, especially after her marriage broke down. Diana learnt an important lesson along the way – you cannot pick and choose when and where you want tabloid attention. Diana announced that she wanted to retire from public life and the paparazzi were furious – her decision would directly affect their bank balances.

Diana wanted to be adored; she yearned for love and affection first from her husband, and then from the British public, and the appetite for information and images of her fuelled the frenzy of photographers that followed her across the world and eventually to Paris.

Ambitious and relentless in their pursuit of the perfect

shot, a line was crossed that night in the tunnel in Paris. The type of person willing to photograph a dead body purely for sensationalist purposes, to be driven by the financial rewards of that photo in that dreadful moment, indicates callousness beyond comprehension.

How far would you go to get what you want? Are you willing to deal with the paps? Brace yourself for the rocky road to fame.

4
The US's Top 20 Celebrities

In the fame game, money talks. But money may not necessarily shout the loudest – Mother Teresa was undoubtedly a celebrity, but had virtually nothing to call her own. When assessing a ranking of top celebrities in the US, many factors are taken into account – earnings, public profile, Internet hits on official websites, mass appeal, media coverage, body of work… and something as basic as their talent for doing what they do and earning money from it. Combine all these factors, and you have a pretty accurate guide of who's hot, and who's not, in the USA.

1: TOM CRUISE
Reputed to have earned around $67 million in 2005–06, The little Big Man of the silver screen tops the polls in

many areas – he's a sofa-hopping Scientologist who's bedded a few of the world's most beautiful women, and can make fans swoon with one flash of his cheesiest smile and buns of steel. His clean-cut, clean-living image has kept the multiplex megastar in the number-one spot in the US celebrity hit parade.

2: THE ROLLING STONES

The band is estimated to have earned around $90 million in 2005–06, with the Stones' A Bigger Bang tour grossing about $162 million by the end of 2005. Any band that can pull in a single audience of 1.5 million – in Rio – has got to be taken seriously, and the English geriatrics are way ahead of all their younger, hungrier and prettier rivals. They've also managed to keep that rock-star edge, which most granddads find a little hard to project. Rather than ending up in hospital for replacement hips or pacemaker fittings, Keith Richards, for example, fell out of a tree in Fiji while he and Ronnie Wood were supposedly trying to get some coconuts. After having his skull drilled to relieve the pressure on his brain, he's expected to make a full recovery. His catchphrase greeting to fans on stage has never been more apt – 'Good to be here… good to be anywhere!' Respect!

3: OPRAH WINFREY

Having amassed something in the region of $225 million in 2005–06, Oprah is the queen of all she surveys, and her multimedia empire is set to take over the world. She's a classy, talented, intelligent, good-looking, mumsy, homespun, humorous, African-American, with the most amazing list of celebrity chums you could ever hope to have. With a prime-time talk show, and hundreds of other projects across various media – theatre, radio, film and TV – she is America's pre-eminent female celebrity, and one of its most powerful movers and shakers. When Oprah says read something from her book club, the world virtually tips on its axis as millions of Americans stampede towards their nearest bookstore. Now *that's* power.

4: U2

The Irish rock gods apparently made more money in 2005 than any other musicians on Earth. But it's Bono – their front man and virtual guru – who is responsible for catapulting them up to number four in the celebrity charts. He has been nominated for a Nobel Peace Prize, is an authority on world poverty and AIDS awareness, and has speed dial numbers for several of the world's most influential statesmen and world leaders on his mobile phone – George W Bush, the late Pope John Paul II, Nelson Mandela – and he's single-handedly responsible for the phenomenal growth in popularity of wrap-around sunglasses.

5: TIGER WOODS

At only number five in the listing, it is perhaps surprising that Tiger is clawing his way to a cool $1 billion in earnings by 2010. And all for hitting a little ball into a hole. He's earned nearly half a billion dollars already from advertising contracts, nearly $100 million from prize winnings, and as he's sickeningly only just in his thirties so he's got plenty of miles left on the clock. And he doesn't just waste his cash on fast cars, private jets and luxury yachts – although he has spent a significant proportion of it on those celebrity essentials. He has also built a $25 million educational facility called the Tiger Woods Education Facility, aimed at encouraging children to get the most out of learning. And it's address is 1, Tiger Woods Way... it's one thing having a school named after you, but to have the road it's in named after you as well, now that's serious celebrity clout!

6: STEVEN SPIELBERG

Around $330 million earned during 2005–06 helps to secure the Oscar-winning director/producer a place among the most powerful players in Hollywood, and one of the most influential business people in America. He's also highly respected among his peers and public alike, and has contributed immeasurably to many charitable and worthwhile causes since he rose to fame as the director of *Duel*, *Jaws*, *ET* and *Jurassic Park*. With a body of work that ranges from a cute little alien to the persecution of the Jewish people in *Schindler's List*, Spielberg can justifiably claim to be one of the greatest living directors of our age.

7: HOWARD STERN

$300 million in a year for being a foul-mouthed, sensationalist, 'shock-jock' DJ seems a little hard to believe, even in the increasingly weird world of celebrity, where there are virtually no rules. But the self-styled 'King of all Media' regularly has over 25 million listeners to his shows, and he's now pioneering satellite radio for Sirius. He's the most fined radio personality in history, claiming that he's not out to shock, but that he merely expresses truth, whether people like it or not. He also claims to be a chronic masturbator, and when he ran for governor of New York in 1994, he promised to restore the death penalty, limit road construction work to night-time hours and abolish tolls.

8: 50 CENT

The guns, the bling, the rap, or the multi-million-dollar corporation that he founded called G Unit... what is it about 50 Cent that makes him such an influential celebrity? At a modest $40 million or so in 2005–06, the rapper's earnings don't really reflect the hold he has over the music business, the potential he could make as an actor, and the sheer volume of his fan base. His last couple of albums have sold around 20 million copies worldwide, and his image – that of a half-naked street fighter with a six-pack torso and a smoking gun – undoubtedly add that essential X factor to his celebrity status. He's loud, controversial, dangerous… and anyone over the age of 30 hates him. But there are enough who love him to keep his celebrity candle burning for a while yet.

9: CAST OF *THE SOPRANOS*

The combined earnings of this team of mega-star actors is around $50 million, with the success of the programme ensuring that the leads have a massive amount of clout in the US television and film industries. James Gandolfini reportedly commands $1 million per episode, and Michael Imperioli, Edie Falco and Lorraine Bracco are all enjoying top-flight careers on other projects thanks to the outrageous exploits of their characters on the show. Who says crime doesn't pay?

10: DAN BROWN

Dan Brown is the author responsible for *The Da Vinci Code*, a book so widespread in its popularity that hotels around the world are thinking of popping it in bedside cabinets instead of the Bible. So far, over 65 million copies have been sold in most of the world's languages. There is so much demand for this book, apparently, that there will soon be an edition available in Klingon. It's a book for which the word 'hype' was invented, and then when the film came out, starring Tom Hanks, Brown's earnings leapt to around $80 million. Whether he can keep it up is another matter. Prepare yourself for *The Constable Code*, *The Lowry Code* and, for those who like to combine their art with their love of pets, *The Rolf Harris Code*.

11: BRUCE SPRINGSTEEN

$55 million in 2005–06, and The Boss is still going strong. Famous for 'finding grandeur in the struggles of everyday life', he's also managed to find loads of cash from singing about it.

12: DONALD TRUMP

Reputedly one of the world's richest businessmen, Trump earned a paltry $44 million in 2005–06, which barely covered the wax polish for his gleaming black private jet. The property tycoon has plenty of sources of income though, most notably his hosting of the US version of *The Apprentice*, and he reportedly commands $1-million attendance fees on the speaker circuit. He endorses several different products, from which he makes a vast amount of money, and which keep him looking and smelling like a very rich celebrity.

13: MUHAMMAD ALI

The boxing legend recently sold the rights to his name and image for $50 million to the chief executive of CKX, whose stable of iconic American brands includes *American Idol* and Elvis Presley. He's also linked to the GOAT brand – he called himself the 'Greatest of All Time – from which Ali gets a percentage of all sales. Ali's power and image transcends racial or cultural boundaries, and he inspired a collective gasp of approval and goodwill from billions of viewers at the Los Angeles Olympics in 1996 when he was unveiled as the surprise celebrity icon who would light the Olympic flame.

14: PAUL McCARTNEY

Earning around £40 million in 2005–06, McCartney is in danger of losing it all, and a couple of hundred million more, if his ex-wife Heather has anything to do with it. But he won't have to busk in Tube stations to make ends meet. He has a reputed fortune of around £850 million to fall back on, and his daughter, Stella, could probably now keep her old man in the style to which he's become accustomed through her successful design business. 'We can work it out... ' he once sang. For the sake of their children, let's hope he does.

15: GEORGE LUCAS

For a director who's responsible for three of the most panned sequels of all time, Lucas isn't doing too badly. Like his films, he doesn't do things by halves, and his

$230 million in 2005–06 shows that however many critics hated his fourth, fifth and sixth – or should that be 'Sith'– *Star Wars* instalments, there are enough geeky computer nerds around to make Lucas a Force to be reckoned with in the celebrity firmament.

16: ELTON JOHN

Whatever list you're compiling – Most Outrageous Catsuit, Queeniest hissy-fit, Most Intricate Hairweave – Elton will always feature. He's a gossip columnist's dream, and he's still loved by a public who are enthralled by his music, and intrigued by his extravagant life-

style. Earning a reputed $34 million in 2005–06, the Rocket Man is now raking it in from his collaborations on musical theatre projects, and winning critical plaudits around the globe for such productions as the *Lion King* and *Billy Elliot*. He also earns around $17 million for his regular appearances Vegas.

17: DAVID LETTERMAN

Late Night with David Letterman reputedly earned the chat-show host $40 million in 2005–06, and he has sufficient clout to attract the biggest and best stars – Oprah Winfrey was a recent guest, and he trumped his rivals – Jay Leno, particularly – when Britney Spears announced her pregnancy on his show. In the world of celebrity, you've not really made it unless you can sit in the company of a similarly top-ranking star, in front of millions of people, and give them intimate details of your inner workings. Another Letterman coup.

18: PHIL MICKELSON

Number 18 in the list, and we've got two golfers already. It just shows you the power of the sport in the public's imagination, and their willingness to follow the fortunes of the greatest drivers, wedgers and putters as they hack their way slowly – sometimes very slowly – around 18 holes. And if you actually go to a tournament, you'll need binoculars, a periscope and twenty-twenty vision to see anything at all. Despite this, Mickelson managed to amass $35 million in 2005–06, and attracts a huge following of devoted fans. He's won majors in three successive years, and has lucrative marketing deals with several well-heeled organisations.

19: J K ROWLING

Is there anyone left on Earth who hasn't heard J K Rowling's name? She is very nearly a billionaire, as she prepares to bring her *Harry Potter* series to an end. The bandwagon, though, is bound to continue for many years to come. With

over 300 million copies sold, and billions of children yearning for boarding school and Potions classes, the films have helped to keep the Potter industry alive in the minds of the public the world over. *The Goblet of Fire* grossed nearly $900 million alone, so the days of Rowling sitting in a café and making a coffee last for a couple of hours are long gone. She now has the buying power of a small country, having weaved her magic across the globe.

20: BRAD PITT

With $25 million in his pocket for 2005–06, and half a billion dollars from *Mr and Mrs Smith* alone, money is the least of Brad's worries. Neither is hanging out with the world's most desirable women. Like London buses, just when you hop off one, another usually turns up hot on its tail. After his split from Jennifer Aniston, he became linked with Angelina Jolie, and then had a child with her, named Shiloh. And in true celebrity style, when they could afford to buy several hospitals in the US to make the labour as painless and as safe as possible, they decided to fly out to Namibia and have the baby there. And they monopolised a hotel and a hospital to do it, and inadvertently forced the Namibian government to make special arrangements for their peace and security to avoid the world's media getting a look in. And they went to Namibia to escape the press, they said. As far as celebrity status goes, things don't get much more A-list than this.

5
Celebrity Tantrums

*'Fame means millions of people have the
wrong idea of who you are.'*
ERICA JONG

Celebrity tantrums (as if you didn't know) are extravagant outbursts by people who are usually regarded as famous... or who regard themselves as famous. They tend to get the desired effect if the celebrity is high profile enough – minions will scurry around after you, no matter how badly they're treated, if you're Maria Callas, for example. But if you're a walk-on part on a cable TV soap opera, then no amount of throwing your toys out of the pram will get you what you want. People will just laugh and never book you again. The bigger the celebrity, the bigger the tantrum... and the bigger the rewards.

Celebrity tantrums are commonly triggered by trivial events and, at best, result in the venting of a bit of frustration, and a reaffirmation that the tantrum-maker is really the centre of the universe; at worst, they can result in cancelled appearances and lawsuits, leaving tens of thousands of people thoroughly cheesed off. Such occurrences are widely reported in the mass media, with some stars gaining a reputation for their tempers. When the celebrity is a female, or if they are possibly homosexual, they are sometimes referred to as a 'diva' – Joan Crawford or Rita Heyworth easily qualified for this title.

While some tantrums appear unjustified and irrational, others are prompted by the continual invasion of privacy that celebrities have to face, particularly from the paparazzi.

The paparazzi have caused, and been the target of, many celebrity tantrums. They often leave celebrities with very little private time, monitoring their every movement.

Elton John has been the subject of various tantrum stories over many years. One such outburst, captured on video and subsequently shown on many television entertainment shows and even some news programmes, happened before a show in Taiwan. He called the assembly of photographers and television crews 'rude, vile pigs' after being upset about their presence and treatment of him. A spokesperson stated that the singer was annoyed by the lack of intervention from the police.

Björk was also famously filmed when she attacked a journalist. In February 1996, Björk arrived at Bangkok airport and was greeted by a French television crew.

The infuriated singer attacked the interviewer.

Justin Timberlake and Cameron Diaz got into a full-on tussle with paps after leaving the Château Marmont Hotel in Hollywood. The November 2004 spat caused headlines and both Diaz and Timberlake went to court over the fracas. Diaz had apparently grabbed the paparazzi's camera, but eventually returned it to the police with all pictures intact. The case was eventually settled out of court.

IRRITATING INTERVIEWERS

The questions from interviewers or the comments of chat-show hosts can easily spark a swift reaction, particularly when the questions become too personal. The Bee Gees walked out during their 1997 appearance on BBC2's *Clive Anderson – All Talk*, when host Clive Anderson made a joke at their expense. Noting that they once considered the name 'Les Tosseurs' for the band, Anderson said to them, 'You'll always be Les Tosseurs to me'. The three of them immediately stood up and left.

Footage of singer Grace Jones slapping TV host Russell Harty is one of the most famous and unsettling displays of a tantrum caused by the questions asked by an interviewer, and was voted 'the most shocking TV chat-show moment of all time' in a poll commissioned by UKTV Gold. There's no doubt in Grace Jones's case, though, that while Harty was clearly not on top form that night as a host, Jones clearly felt that actions spoke louder than words that evening.

One frequent cause of celebrity tantrums is the inclusion of various 'riders' on celebrity contracts – these are the unique requirements or stipulations which a celebrity demands if they are to play ball, and they can range from requiring a red carpet lined with flaming torches at the entrance to every hotel on arrival, to having their dressing room painted a particular shade of lilac.

One of the earliest examples of an unusual rider was Van Halen's 'Article 126', known as 'the brown M&M clause'. This led to David Lee Roth (the lead singer of the group) trashing the backstage area of the University of Pueblo, Colorado, when he spotted brown M&Ms in a large bowl. The media exaggerated the scale of the damage, stating it to be $85,000, while the band claimed it to be nearer $12,000. The management of the group also explained the reasoning for such an unusual clause – it was used to check up on how well the organisers had read through the contract, with the assumption that if they had missed Article 126, they could miss other, more important parts.

Listed below are some of the standard riders demanded by our best-loved celebrity divas:

BON JOVI

Jon and his mates requested one gallon of chocolate milk and a large urn of chicken noodle soup. Who said rock 'n' roll is dead?

MARILYN MANSON

450g block of extra-sharp cheddar
450g block of Swiss, Gouda or Munster cheese
4 bags of Haribo Gold Gummi Bears.
1 bottle Absinthe
5kg fresh minced beef (for those emergency I-need-beef moments)

ROLLING STONES

Full-size snooker table
A pinball machine
A ping-pong table

JENNIFER LOPEZ

White room
White flowers
White tables
White curtains
White candles
White couches
White lilies
White roses

MADONNA

A brand new toilet seat – the seat has to be inspected by her people, then installed – with an unbroken seal – by plumbers before every gig
A DNA of the Soul candle

A Power of Prosperity candle
An Evil Eye candle
An Ein Gedi Dead Sea Foot Spa
Kabbalah water
An all-white dressing room
White roses

PRINCE

The Purple One may be going the way of notorious clean-freaks Kim and Aggie from TV's *How Clean Is Your House?* His rider states that 'all items in the dressing room must be wrapped in clear plastic until uncovered by main artist.' Let's just hope he remembers to take the Cellophane off the loo.

WHEN TANTRUMS GO BAD

Some celebrities can still surprise you, just when you think you've got them safely in the right pigeon hole. Who'd have thought that Mel Gibson, who'd served his time as a hell-raising, hard-drinking macho star in *Mad Max*, and who had now become one of Hollywood's most bankable and permanent fixtures, expounding decent, Christian family values, would be capable of saying, in public, 'The Jews are responsible for all the wars in the world...' and then yelling at a female police sergeant, 'What do you think you're looking at, sugar tits?'

Following his anti-Semitic tirade, and acknowledging that it's really immaterial whether a policewoman's tits are sugary or otherwise, Mel Gibson has tried every route possible – once he'd sobered up – to say he's sorry. He even asked the Jewish community – most of whom were pretty much convinced of his anti-Semitic beliefs anyway with his 2004 film *The Passion of the Christ*, and for his refusal to distance himself from his Holocaust-denying father – 'to help [him] on his journey through recovery'.

Is this sufficient to salvage his career? Only time – and future box-office takings for Mel Gibson films – will tell. If history can teach Gibson anything, it's that a choreographed tour of heartfelt remorse, and a well-crafted PR campaign, can save almost anyone. Until we hear the verdict on Mel, here are ten other celebrity mishaps that once rocked the tabloids.

FATTY ARBUCKLE, COMEDIAN AND ACTOR

This vaudeville-heavyweight-turned-silent-film star was, in his day, even more popular than Charlie Chaplin. In 1921, he signed a then-whopping $1-million-a-year contract with Paramount Pictures, but at a drunken party celebrating the deal, starlet Virginia Rappe was found dead. Arbuckle was accused of her rape and murder.

Arbuckle maintained his innocence through three trials. When he was finally acquitted, the jury apologised to him. 'Acquittal is not enough for Roscoe Arbuckle,' it wrote in its decision. 'We feel that a great injustice has been done him... There was not the slightest proof adduced to connect him in any way with the commission of a crime.'

Pal Buster Keaton sent some directing work Arbuckle's way (which the latter did under a pseudonym), but the actor was essentially blacklisted and never recovered from the scandal. He died of heart failure in 1933, at the age of 46, following years of heroin and alcohol abuse.

ROMAN POLANSKI, FILM DIRECTOR

In 1977, the legendary director of *Chinatown* and *Rosemary's Baby* pleaded guilty to having sex with a 13-year-old girl.

There never was an apology. To avoid a likely jail sentence, Polanski fled to Paris. At the time, he refused to speak to the press, but court reports noted that he was distraught over the 1969 murder of his wife, Sharon Tate, who was killed by followers of Charles Manson. Sources also said that Polanski – a survivor of the Krakow ghetto and Auschwitz – couldn't bear the thought of being locked up.

Polanski remains in exile in France. His controversial history was stirred up in 2003, when he received an Oscar for Best Director for his film *The Pianist*. Although he didn't risk attending the ceremony in person, Polanski did receive support from an unlikely source – his victim, Samantha Geimer. Now in her early 40s, she went public, urging the world to 'judge the movie, not the man'.

ROB LOWE, ACTOR

In 1989, the 24-year-old Brat Packer faced a civil lawsuit and a criminal investigation after the release of a videotape showing him having sex with a woman and a 16-year-old girl during the Democratic convention in Atlanta a year earlier.

The civil case was settled out of court, and Lowe performed community service to avoid charges of sexually exploiting a minor. 'I could be the poster boy for bad judgement,' Lowe told the media.

The rising star spent close to a decade in D-list purgatory, the low point being an Oscar-night performance of *Proud Mary* with Snow White. His career rehabilitation began with cameo performances in *Wayne's World* and *Austin Powers: The Spy Who Shagged Me*. He confirmed his comeback playing over-achieving deputy communications director Sam Seaborn in the Emmy-winning drama *West Wing*. The pilot featured Sam caught in a characteristically racy clinch – he had a one-night stand with a woman who turned out to be a high-priced Beltway call girl.

HUGH GRANT, ACTOR

In 1995, fresh from his first US box-office hit, *Four Weddings and a Funeral*, the stuttering toff with the

floppy hair was caught having something else made a little less floppy in a car, his pants around his ankles and prostitute Divine Brown's gums around his plums.

Two weeks after his arrest for 'lewd behaviour', Grant made a tail-between-the-legs *mea culpa* tour, promoting two new films – *Nine Months* and *An Awfully Big Adventure* – on *Live with Regis and Kathie Lee*, *The Tonight Show* and *Larry King Live*. He was duly contrite as he apologised to fans and long-time girlfriend, Elizabeth Hurley; he called his behaviour 'disloyal and shabby and goatish'. He did slip in one quip, though, telling Jay Leno, 'I've never been one to, you know, blow my own trumpet.'

Hurley eventually kicked Grant out of her life, but his career took an upswing when he trimmed his foppish hair, dropped the Jimmy Stewart gosh-golly stammer and embraced his dark side. His turns as self-absorbed cads in *Bridget Jones's Diary* and *About a Boy* are two of his best and funniest performances.

EDDIE MURPHY, COMEDIAN AND ACTOR

In 1997, Murphy was stopped by police in a pre-dawn bust of a transvestite prostitute named Antisone Seiuli. Police had been watching Seiuli when Murphy picked the hooker up in a well-known sex-trade district of Hollywood.

Murphy blamed his late-night drive on a bout of insomnia and said he was just a Good Samaritan trying to help what he thought was a female prostitute by giving her a ride home. He told *People* magazine that it was 'an act of kindness that got turned into a fucking horror show'.

There was hardly any fallout from this, though. The formerly foul-mouthed Murphy had already begun to reinvent himself when the story broke as a PG-rated star in films like *The Nutty Professor. Dr Doolittle*, the first Murphy film to be released after the story broke, was a hit, grossing more than $140 million in the US.

WINONA RYDER, ACTRESS

In 2001, the Oscar-winning starlet was arrested at an upmarket boutique in Beverly Hills with $5,500 worth of stolen merchandise. She was later sentenced to three years' probation and 480 hours of community service.

During the trial, a store security guard testified that Ryder told him, 'I'm sorry for what I did. My director directed me to shoplift for a role.'

Her waning career was given a boost when Ryder became a cool *cause célèbre* with a 'Free Winona' T-shirt campaign. She even wore one herself on the cover of *W* magazine and while hosting an episode of *Saturday Night Live*. Ryder's film career also received a much needed boost when she appeared in Richard Linklater's *A Scanner Darkly*, and there is talk that she will reunite some time soon with *Heathers* screenwriter-turned-director Daniel Waters for the film *Sex and Death 101*.

MICHAEL JACKSON, SINGER

It's difficult to pick just one episode when looking at Michael Jackson's career and increasingly weird lifestyle... not to mention the scandal of his sledgehammered face.

In 1993, a 14-month police investigation into allegations of child molestation came up with no charges. That same year, Jackson settled a civil suit out of court in which he'd been accused of abusing a 13-year-old boy.

In 2002, he dangled his baby Prince Michael II (otherwise known as 'Blanket') from a Berlin hotel balcony. The following year, he was charged with molesting a 13-year-old cancer patient.

Jackson admitted to making a 'terrible mistake' in dangling his son over a hotel balcony, but contended that his relationships with young boys – which included regular sleepovers – were perfectly innocent.

Jackson's bizarre trial was upstaged by the singer's even more extraordinary antics, which included dancing to his own music atop a SUV outside the courthouse. To the glee of his fans, he was acquitted of all charges in 2005 and has since spent much of his time in self-imposed exile in Dubai.

KATE MOSS, MODEL

In 2005, after years of being blamed for popularising the skin-and-bones aesthetic dubbed 'heroin chic', a British tabloid published a photograph of the catwalking party girl snorting cocaine at a recording studio. She'd been visiting then-boyfriend and Babyshambles front man Pete Doherty, himself a walking pharmacy.

Moss apologised to 'all the people I have let down' and promptly entered a rehab clinic. The fallout has been minimal and, if anything, Moss's career has gone from strength to a minor blip, to even more strength. Most of her big fashion house bosses dropped Moss as a model but, soon after, she signed new deals with Calvin Klein and Virgin Mobile. She has since graced the covers of just about every magazine (both in the US and UK), including *Vanity Fair*. Moss's on-off relationship with Pete Doherty seems to have continued, too, with the tabloids fighting over pictures of the two of them being seen out together. One celeb going off the rails is great, but two is dynamite.

6
Reality Television

*'Television is more interesting than people.
If it were not, we should have people standing
in the corner of our room.'*
ALAN COREN

In the beginning there was a box. Inside the box there were glass valves that gave off a ghostly yellow glow. There was a screen which flickered black and white. There was one channel and it was good. It was 1936.

In the pioneering days of television, you would settle down in front of the little fuzzy image with your entire family, and watch wholesome, uncontroversial fare such as *Muffin the Mule* or *Gone with the Wind*. And during the breaks, you could enjoy the potter's wheel, or watch the test card with the little girl and her clown. Television was all about escapism, fantasy, and was as far removed from reality as you can get – apart from when the BBC transmitter went down.

'Reality' television is a nebulous concept. Supposedly, it is the watching of individuals – celebrity or otherwise – in 'real' situations, behaving and reacting in a 'real' way to 'real' circumstances without a script. Although how close to 'reality' the enforced mania of Big Brother really is, or how 'real' the tropical nut-house of *Celebrity Love Island* is, is open to debate. A lot of debate.

There are a number of forerunners to our modern-day reality shows, starting as far back as the 1950s. Allen Funt's television show *Candid Camera*, which made a debut in 1953 (and itself was based on his previous 1947 radio show, *Candid Microphone*), played pranks on unsuspecting 'ordinary' members of the public and recorded their reactions. It has been called the 'grandaddy of the reality TV genre'. Another predecessor was the BBC series *Seven Up!* which was first broadcast in the UK in 1964. The series chronicles the growth, attitudes and development of a dozen ordinary seven-year-olds from a broad cross-section of society, and their responses to questions on everyday life. Then, every seven years, a follow-up film is made catching up with the same individuals and filling the viewer in on the intervening years, titled *Seven Plus Seven*, *21 Up*, and so on. The series cannot truly be classified as 'reality television' because it is structured simply as a series of interviews, with no element of recording the individuals' reactions or behaviour in ordinary, everyday situations; it did, though, pioneer the concept of making television celebrities out of ordinary people.

The first reality show in the modern sense was the PBS series *An American Family*. Twelve parts were broadcast in the United States in 1973. The series dealt with a nuclear family going through a divorce. In 1974, a counterpart programme, *The Family*, was made in the UK, following the working-class Wilkins family of Reading. In 1992, Australia saw *Sylvania Waters*, about the *nouveau riche* Baker-Donaher family of Sydney. All three shows attracted their share of controversy.

Some talk shows, most notably *The Jerry Springer Show*, which made a debut in 1991, try to present real-life drama within the talk-show format by putting on guests likely to get into fights with one another on the set. That combination of highly emotive subjects – *Your Girlfriend is a Secret Transsexual* or *I Want My Granny to Stop Lap Dancing* – along with a general level of IQ among the guests that would make Jade Goody look like Einstein, means that this 'reality' talk-show format can still pull in the viewers in their millions, and at least one really good verbal or physical assault can be guaranteed in a half-hour slot. And if there are two or three, and perhaps the break-up of a marriage, then so much the better.

Reality television as it is currently understood, though, can be traced directly to several television shows that began in the late 1980s and 1990s. *COPS*, which was first aired in 1989, showed police officers on duty apprehending criminals; it introduced the shaky camcorder style and *cinéma vérité* feel of much of later reality television.

MTV's *The Real World*, which began in 1992, originated the concept of putting strangers together in the same environment for an extended period of time and recording the drama that ensued. It also pioneered many of the stylistic conventions that have since become standard in reality television shows, including a heavy use of soundtrack music and the interspersing of events on screen with after-the-fact 'confessionals' recorded by cast members that serve as narration.

Changing Rooms began in 1996, showing couples redecorating each others' houses, and was the first reality show with a self-improvement or makeover theme. The Swedish TV show *Expedition Robinson*, which was first aired in 1997 (and was later produced in a large number of other countries as *Survivor*), added to the 'real world' template the idea of competition, in which cast members/contestants battled against each other and were removed from the show until only one winner remained. The Australian series *The House from Hell* in 1998, hosted by Andrew Denton and Amanda Keller on Network Ten, was possibly the first example of a *Big Brother* style show.

DOCUMENTARY STYLE

In many reality television shows, the viewer and the camera are passive observers following people going about their daily personal and professional activities; this style of filming is often referred to as 'fly on the wall' or *cinéma vérité*. MTV's *Laguna Beach: The Real*

Orange County may be the epitome of this style of show, with unscripted situations, real-life locations, and no predetermined tasks given to the cast (at least, no known ones).

Often 'plots' are constructed via editing or planned situations, so that the results resemble soap operas – hence the term 'docusoap'.

SPECIAL LIVING ENVIRONMENT

Some documentary-style programmes place cast members, who often previously did not know each other, in artificial living environments; *The Real World* is the originator of this style. In almost every other such show, cast members are given a specific challenge or obstacle to overcome. *Road Rules*, which started in 1995 as a spin-off of *The Real World*, started this pattern. The cast travelled across the country guided by clues and performing tasks.

Many other shows in this category involve historical re-enactment, with cast members forced to live and work as people of a specific time and place; *The 1900 House* is one example. *Temptation Island* in 2001 achieved some notoriety by placing several couples on an island surrounded by single people in order to test the couples' commitment to each other, and to enjoy the sight of gorgeous, supermodel-style guys and gals succumbing to temptation and ruining their relationships with long-term partners. All this with a tropical backdrop and some tears and arguments thrown in – fantastic!

CELEBRITY REALITY

Another collection of fly-on-the-wall-style shows involves celebrities. Often, these follow a celebrity going about their everyday life; examples include *The Anna Nicole Show*, *The Osbournes*, and *Newlyweds* (featuring Jessica Simpson and Nick Lachey). In other shows, celebrities are put on location and given a specific task or tasks to do. These include *The Simple Life* and ITV's *I'm a Celebrity – Get Me Out of Here!* VH1 has created an entire block of shows dedicated to celebrity reality called *celebreality*.

PROFESSIONAL ACTIVITIES

Some documentary-style shows portray professionals either going about their day-to-day business, or performing an entire project over the course of a series. No external experts are brought in (at least, none of them show up on screen) to either provide help or to judge results.

The earliest and best known of these is *COPS*. Another example is *The Restaurant*, which covered the creation and running of a restaurant. VH1's 2001 show *Bands on the Run* was a notable early hybrid, in that the show featured four unsigned bands touring and making music as a professional activity, but also pitted the bands against one another in game-show fashion to see which band could make the most money.

GAME SHOWS

Another type of reality TV is so-called 'reality game shows', in which participants are filmed competing to win a prize, usually while living together. Probably the purest example of a reality game show is the globally syndicated *Big Brother* – no skills are involved in winning the show other than being appealing to others and handling the dynamics of a group well. *Unan1mous* is another example.

There remains controversy over whether talent-search shows such as the *Idol* series, *The X Factor, So You Think You Can Dance, Dancing with the Stars*, and *Skating with Celebrities* are truly reality television, or just newer incarnations of shows such as *Star Search*. There is no element of plot on these shows; on the other hand, there is a good deal of interaction shown between contestants and judges, and the shows follow the traditional reality-game show conventions of removing one contestant per episode and empowering the viewers by offering the opportunity to phone in or text in their least favourite, who ends up being dumped.

A twist to this, which ended up in court, was when producers of the UK's *Big Brother* 7 reinstated one contestant – Nikki – after she had been thrown out by the public. This was later investigated by a television watchdog, who ruled that Channel 4 had broken their agreement with the public, who had paid through their calls and texts for Nikki to be removed. Channel 4 admitted liability, and paid all the court costs, but the real winner was Nikki. Having enjoyed her 15 minutes of fame, and then having been given another bite of the celebrity cherry, she has now landed her own show on E4 called *Princess Nikki*, in which she is set the task of holding down a variety of 'proper jobs'. Presumably, being talented at anything is not part of the job description.

Modern game shows like *The Weakest Link*, *Who Wants to Be a Millionaire?*, *Dog Eat Dog*, *Deal or No Deal* and *Fear Factor* also lie in a grey area. Like traditional game shows, the action usually takes place in an enclosed TV studio over a short period of time. *Deal or No Deal* is, of course, one of the most successful formats of modern television, and has attracted a cult following, although how many viewers are tuning in to see Noel Edmonds, or are genuinely interested in seeing a nonentity win up to £250,000, is anybody's guess.

These game shows tend to have very high-level production values, more dramatic background music, and higher stakes, either through putting contestants into apparent physical danger or upping the risk through high cash prizes. There also tends to be more interaction between contestants and hosts and, in some cases, such as *The Weakest Link*, *Dog Eat Dog* or *Fear Factor*, reality-style contestant elimination as well.

There are various hybrids, like the worldwide-syndicated *Star Academy*, which combines the *Big Brother* and *Pop Idol* formats; *The Biggest Loser*, which combines competition with the self-improvement format; and *American Inventor*, which uses the *Pop Idol* format for products instead of people. Some shows, such as *Making the Band* and *Project Green Light*, devote the first part of the season to selecting a winner, and the second part to showing that person or group of people working at what it was they were selected to do.

DATING-BASED COMPETITION

Dating-based competition shows follow a contestant choosing the hand of a group of suitors. Over the course of the season, the suitors are eliminated one by one until the end, when only the contestant and the final suitor remains. *The Bachelor* is the best-known member of this genre, although one of the most entertaining twists on this format in 2003–05 was *Playing It Straight*, in which a girl – suitably gorgeous, obviously – has to spend some time with a group of twelve men, some of whom are gay. She gets to eliminate one guy per episode, but there's a catch – if she manages to weed out all the gay guys, and ends up with a straight partner, she'll win £100,000. If, however, she ends up with a gay guy, *he* wins all the money. So it's a show with a lot of oiled up biceps, six-packs and pectorals, and making sure that you're mucho macho, and not queenily camp. As dating reality shows go, the female's contestant's dilemmas over who is gay, and the gay guys' desperation to appear perfectly at home with beers, power tools and talk about tits and bums, made this stand out in a packed market.

JOB SEARCH

In this category, the competition revolves around a skill that contestants are pre-screened for. Competitors perform a variety of tasks based around that skill, and are judged, and then kept or removed, by a single expert or a panel of experts. The show is invariably presented as a job search of some kind, in which the prize for the winner includes a contract to perform that kind of work. Hugely successful examples include *America's Next Top Model* and *Project Runway*. Another version of this style of 'job-search game show' is *The Apprentice*, in which super-ambitious young business professionals compete to win a job as a £100,000-a-year gofer for a multimillionaire. In the UK, Sir Alan Sugar has barked 'You're fired!' over the course of several series, and in the States, Martha Stewart and Donald Trump have been doing the firing and hiring.

SPORTS

These programmes create a sporting competition among participants who are athletes attempting to establish their name in that sport. *The Big Break* is one such show for golfing wannabes, and *The Contender*, a boxing show, became the first American reality show in which a contestant committed suicide after being eliminated from the show. One aspect of reality television that perhaps hasn't been developed as fully as the programmes themselves is what happens to the participants when the cameras stop rolling, and whether contestants are psychologically robust enough to cope with the repercussions of failure, or winning. In each season of *The Ultimate Fighter*, at least one participant has voluntarily withdrawn or expressed the desire to withdraw from the show due to competitive pressure.

SELF-IMPROVEMENT/MAKEOVER

Some reality TV shows cover a person or group of people improving some part of their lives. The British show *Changing Rooms*, which began in 1996, was the first such show, although 'improvement' is sometimes debatable. Memorable episodes include Laurence Llewelyn-Bowen designing a purple-and-black bedroom which left the owner speechless, and then sobbing her heart out in shock, and the one in which Handy Andy decided to build some suspended shelving for the owners' prized collection of china teapots. Unfortunately, the shelving did not remain suspended for very long, and a unique, prized collection of broken china was instantly created.

Sometimes, the same group of people are followed over an entire season (as in *The Swan* and *Celebrity Fit Club*), but usually there is a new target for improvement in each episode. Despite differences in the content, the format is usually the same – first the show introduces the subject in their natural environment, and shows us the less-than-ideal conditions they are currently in. In the case of *Honey, We're Killing the Kids*, the twist is that you see the current effects of an over-indulgent lifestyle – obese, jaded, vacant or highly aggressive children – and then 'experts' project their physical image forward by twenty to thirty years. The shock of seeing their little treasures as wasted, slack-bottomed tubs of lard, who seem destined for drug addiction and a lengthy stay at Her Majesty's Pleasure, invariably catapults the parents into becoming acquainted with a whole new approach to life – vegetables and exercise. Over the ensuing four weeks, the impact of those haunting images is minimised, and they get a chance to see what the super-computer predicts for their reformed offspring. Smiley, clear-skinned, thinner faces seem to prove the benefits of turning your back on two litres of Coke and several packets of crisps a day, and another makeover show is successfully over.

In most of these type of shows, the 'victim' meets a group of experts, who give them instructions on how to improve things; they offer aid and encouragement along the way. Finally, the subjects are placed back in their environment and they, along with their friends and family and the experts, appraise the changes that have occurred. Examples of self-improvement or makeover shows include, besides the previously mentioned ones, *The Biggest Loser* (which covers weight loss), *Extreme Makeover* (entire physical appearance), *Life Laundry* (de-junking and de-cluttering one's home, and one's emotional baggage with it), *Queer Eye for the Straight Guy* (style, grooming, interior decoration and cooking skills), *Supernanny* (child rearing), and *Made* (attaining difficult goals).

One show in particular has morphed into another, with the presenters moving from a straight makeover format to a much more profound area of lifestyle and relationship reassessment. Trinny and Susannah fronted *What Not to Wear* for several seasons, in which their subjects were given advice – bordering on bullying, in some cases, with several victim's boobs and buttocks being manhandled with gusto – about their image and appearance. As this often went to the heart of their self-image as well, many more issues were uncovered than one might expect from a pure makeover programme. Now Trinny and Susannah have their own new series – *Trinny and Susannah Undress* – which aims to help subjects 'perk up their wardrobe and put new spark into their relationships'. Quite a feat in an hour slot on ITV, with about 12 minutes given over to adverts.

As with game shows, a grey area exists between such reality TV shows and more conventional formats. The show *This Old House*, which began in 1979, for example, shows people renovating a house. This sort of 'thrilling' format has less and less place on television nowadays, as it requires viewers to tune in regularly over a long period of time, and emotional impact is thin on the ground. Similarly, more recently *Pimp My Ride* and *Overhaulin'* are reality shows depicting vehicles being given dynamic makeovers. It's *Changing Rooms* for petrol-heads. But such shows are generally not considered true reality television because there is little potential for human drama in the format. As we become used to the short-term, emotional impact of modern reality television, the viewer might be forgiven for praying that a stray blow torch is left too near a gas cylinder, or that a minor hiccup with some safety equipment brings steel bars crashing down around workmen's ears. If these programmes are to compete in a highly saturated marketplace, then they'll have to find sufficient 'extraordinary' moments to keep the viewers tuned in.

Unfortunately, real life is just not interesting enough when you let it happen at its own pace, without some sort of drastic intervention, be it Trinny and Susannah jiggling a 60-year-old's breasts, or an entire collection of teapots crashing to the ground in someone's living room.

DATING SHOWS

Some shows, such as *Blind Date*, show people going out on dates. Sometimes a competition element is included, with more than one suitor for each potential match. Antecedents may be found in *The Dating Game* from the 1960s. In 2004, Simon Cowell attempted to reinvent the dating format in the US with his *Cupid* show. Alas, it didn't have the X factor and wasn't a hit, but he still has a couple of other projects to keep his private jet fuelled and ready for take-off.

TALK SHOWS

Though the traditional format of a 'talk show' is that of a host interviewing a featured guest or discussing a chosen topic with a guest or panel of guests, the advent of 'trash' TV shows has often made people group the entire category in with reality television. Programmes like *Ricki Lake*, *The Jerry Springer Show* and others generally recruited everyday guests by advertising a potential topic that producers were working on for a future programme. Topics are frequently outrageous and are chosen in the interest of creating on-screen drama, tension or odd behaviour. Titles such as *I'm in Love with My Uncle*, *Please Dominate Me!* and *My Mom's a Drunk* leave little to the imagination. Though not explicitly reality television by traditional standards, this (allegedly) real depiction of someone's life, even if only in a brief interview format, is frequently considered akin to broader-scale reality TV programming.

'Reality' programming, though, has been questioned in many quarters, particularly where the talk show format is concerned. Perhaps more than any other, talk shows and their producers have sometimes been accused of using actors instead of 'real' guests, when they simply cannot find sufficient contributors for a particular issue. The faking of reality television thus undermines the format, and allows questions to be raised over the credibility and authenticity of its aims, although if the viewer is still getting his or her kicks out of watching bikini-clad transsexuals scratching each other's eyes out over a drug-pushing boyfriend, then does it really matter if they're 'real' or not?

HIDDEN CAMERAS

Another type of reality programming features hidden cameras rolling when random passers-by encounter a staged situation. The reactions of the innocent observers can be funny to watch, but also reveal truths about the human condition. Allen Funt, an American pioneer in reality entertainment, led the way in the development of this type of show.

He created *Candid Microphone*, which made it debut on the ABC Radio Network in 1947, and the internationally successful *Candid Camera*, which was first aired on television in 1953. Modern variants of this type of production include *Punk'd* and the British *Trigger Happy TV*, which stages humorous and/or bizarre situations such as actors in animal costumes pretending to copulate on a crowded sidewalk, or staging mock fights between Dom Joly, the presenter, and apparently random members of the public, while he tries to interview celebrities. The Sci-Fi series *Scare Tactics* is a horror-based hidden-camera show where people can sign up their friends to be scared horrifically.

Perhaps the extreme of this type of candid-camera

entertainment was a show in Brazil that pushed the boundaries of acceptable 'tomfoolery' to an absolute limit. In one scenario, the 'victim' wandered into a cubicle in the Gents toilet at an airport in São Paulo, and proceeded to answer his call of nature. At this point, a couple of actors came into the toilets, and staged a mock drug deal which went wrong, ending up with a 'shooting' of one of them. Overhearing all this, the 'victim' emerges from his cubicle to be confronted with a 'dead' body, and the murder weapon close at hand. The toilet is then invaded by armed police, who immediately assume that our 'victim' is responsible for the shooting. They then make him suffer several minutes of abject terror as he tries to explain his way out of it. And then, lo and behold, the presenter of the show wanders into the toilet, and exposes it all as a hilarious joke. The most surprising thing about this is that no one has shot the presenter yet.

On another occasion, a fake doctor's surgery is set up in a reputable part of town, and women are invited to attend free health screenings. One after another, they are ushered into the doctor's surgery, where they have a brief chat with the 'doctor', who tells them to strip completely and lie on a bed while he wanders out to get some notes. As the 'victims' lie naked on the bed, the walls of the room suddenly shoot up into the ceiling, revealing the fact that the surgery was just a makeshift set in a massive TV studio, and there is a full audience ready and waiting, screaming with laughter at the acute embarrassment of the naked women. Television doesn't get much more entertaining than that!

HOAXES

In hoax reality shows, the entire show is a prank played on one or more of the cast members, who think they are appearing in a legitimate reality show, while the rest of the cast are actors who are in on the joke. Like hidden-camera shows, these shows are about pulling pranks on people, although in these shows the hoax is more elaborate, often lasting an entire season, and the cameras are out in the open.

Also, the point of such shows often is to parody the conventions of the reality TV genre. The first such show was 2003's *The Joe Schmo Show*; other examples are *My Big Fat Obnoxious Boss* (modelled after *The Apprentice*), and *Space Cadets*, which persuaded the hoax targets that they were being trained at a secret Russian cosmonaut facility, and then blasted off into space. To get over the fact they might have wondered about the rather strange phenomenon of gravity in space, they were told that a new anti-gravity device had been fitted on the spaceship. Naturally, it was so hush-hush that none of them would have heard about it beforehand. Although the format sounds as though it could have been quite groundbreaking and intriguing, Channel 4 managed to make quite a sexy format seem very dull, to the point that viewers were left wondering, 'So what?'

Other shows, though they have not gone to the

length of hiring actors, have offered misleading information to some cast members in order to spice up the competition. Examples include *Boy Meets Boy* and *Joe Millionaire*.

REALITY BITES

Part of reality television's appeal is down to its ability to place ordinary people in extraordinary situations – and then hope they perform. For example, on the ABC show *The Bachelor*, an eligible male dates a dozen women simultaneously, travelling on extraordinary dates to the Napa Valley, California and Vail, Colorado. Reality television also has the potential to turn its participants into national celebrities, either because they have participated in a talent show, such as *Pop Idol*, or because they have made a particular impact through the force of their personalities, on shows such as *Survivor* and *Big Brother*.

For many viewers, it is satisfying to know that someone they've seen grow from a nonentity, just like themselves, has the staying power to appear in other shows because of that first moment of exposure. Chantelle on *Celebrity Big Brother* is a case in point – she was the only non-celebrity on the show, and has now eclipsed several of them by remaining in the public eye ever since, and dating a co-celebrity from the show. Viewers everywhere could be heard whispering, 'Well, if it can happen to her…'

The name 'reality television' can be misleading for

several styles of programme routinely included in the genre. In competition-based programmes such as *Big Brother* and *Survivor*, the producers design the format of the show and control the day-to-day activities and the environment, creating a completely fabricated world in which the competition plays out. Producers specifically select the participants, and use carefully designed scenarios, challenges, events and settings to encourage particular behaviours and conflicts.

Even in docusoap series following people in their daily lives, producers have a great deal of influence over the finished product through their editing strategies, and are able to portray certain participants as heroes or villains, and may guide the drama through altered chronology and selective presentation of events. Some participants have stated afterwards that they altered their behaviour to appear more crazy or emotional in order to get more camera time. Yet there has been no clear indication that these programmes are fully scripted or 'rigged,' as with the 1950s television quiz-show scandals, which culminated in the six-figure sums being handed out to the 'winners' of the rigged *Twenty-One*.

Several former reality-show participants have spoken publicly about their experiences and the strategies used on reality shows. With nothing else better to do, Irene McGee from *The Real World Seattle* has undertaken public-speaking tours about the negative and misleading aspects of reality TV. In 2004, VH1 aired a programme called *Reality TV Secrets Revealed* that detailed various misleading tricks of reality TV producers. It was revealed that programmes such as *The Restaurant* and *Survivor* had, at times, recreated incidents that had actually occurred but were not properly recorded by cameras to the required technical standard, or had not been recorded at all. In order to get the footage, the event was restaged for the cameras. Other shows (most notably *Joe Millionaire*) combined audio and video from different times, or different sets of footage, to make it look as though participants were doing something that they actually hadn't ever done.

Reality television will always attract criticism from those who feel that the pervasiveness of the genre on network television has come at the cost of scripted programming. There has also been concern in the media by envious network executives that such programming is limited in its appeal for DVD reissue and syndication, although it remains hugely lucrative for short-term profits, particularly through telephone voting revenues. One series in particular defies this analysis – *COPS* has had huge success in syndication and on DVD. It has been a FOX staple since 1989, and is currently in its 19th season, defying all odds. In late 2004–early 2005, the genre's popularity seemed to be waning in America, with long-running reality shows such as *The Apprentice* scoring lower-than-expected ratings.

The Will became one of a handful of series in television history to be cancelled after only one broadcast. In the show, a wealthy patriarch oversees a competition among several of his would-be heirs to give away a significant portion of his estate. A series of challenges eliminates the heirs one by one, with the last person left collecting the inheritance. How this lame duck of a show ever got the green light in the first place remains a mystery.

However, this may have been only a temporary blip in the popularity of the genre; the finale of VH1's *Flavour of Love* drew 6 million viewers in 2006, making it the highest-rated show in the history of that network. The concept was fairly tame considering the ratings – the actor Flavor Flav assembled 20 girls and set them tasks; the last one standing would then win the opportunity to become his soulmate, and share in the untold riches and excitement of being attached to an A-list celeb. Unfortunately for Flavor – and fortunately for producers of the show – the winner from the first series, Hoopz, decided that pursuing her career as a model and actress was far more enticing than pursuing Flavor, so once the cameras stopped rolling, she was off. Hence series number 2. Let's hope he doesn't end up jumping through more Hoopz.

Similarly, UPN's number one-rated show in 2006 was the reality show *America's Next Top Model*. And in March 2006, a fifth-season episode of *American Idol* drew some of the show's best ratings yet, overshadowing even the 2006 Winter Olympics. An average of 35 million viewers watched each episode with 54 million tuning in to watch the final. Simon Cowell and Simon Fuller have a lot to answer for.

One thing is certain – reality television is set to continue for some time yet. So here's your chance for instant stardom – stock up on fake tan and get your bags packed, as you never know when reality TV will strike.

MOST POPULAR US REALITY TV PROGRAMMES

American Idol
The hit FOX musical reality series in which three judges – Simon Cowell, Randy Jackson (II), and Paula Abdul, along with host Ryan Seacrest – travel around the United States in search of the next bona fide American pop star. The big, fat momma of all talent shows.

America's Got Talent
Not surprisingly, this show's very similar to *American Idol* and – surprise, surprise – it's produced by Simon Cowell and the producers of *Idol*. Here, though, any talent – or lack of it – goes, and a whole variety of acts are encouraged to appear: singing, dancing, magic, comedy, bands, animal acts and bizarre novelty acts are part and parcel of the show's appeal. Like *Idol*, TV viewers choose the best acts... and maximise the profits for the producers though the cost of their calls.

Unlike *Idol*, though, the winner isn't promised fame or a specific performing contract, although that is a likely outcome. What is certain is that they will win a decent chunk of cash to the tune of $1 million. Not bad if you're the best in your region at yodelling or baton twirling.

The Apprentice

For the honour of working for Donald Trump and a six-figure sum 18 ambitious hopefuls compete against each other. They have to endure sly, underhand tactics from fellow competitors, and the critical comments of Trump's two henchmen, who watch their every move. After several series, viewers could be forgiven for responding to Trump's 'You're fired!' with 'Yeah... and we're *tired*!'

America's Next Top Model

Combining the cut and thrust of the cattiest catwalk models, with the possibility of glimpsing a significant amount of voluptuous naked flesh, the show pits 14 wannabe supermodels against each other for a supremely grand prize – an opportunity to be managed by Ford Models, a fashion spread in *Elle* magazine, and a $100,000 contract with *CoverGirl*. But you have to sell your soul to do it, and be prepared to be snapped, probed and ogled every minute of every day.

Participants are assessed on their inner and outer beauty as they master complicated catwalks, intense physical fitness, fashion photo shoots and publicity skills, all under 24-hour-a-day surveillance. And to think that the runner-up goes through all that and gets nothing! Shame.

The Bachelor

One man... 25 women... will he find the woman of his dreams, and will she accept his offer of a relationship?

The gradual process of elimination, and the real blossoming of some true-romance-style friendships and then intimacies, makes this show one of the most popular ever. As the body count rises – with the single women being voted off each week – so the tension is racked up, and the time, effort and emotional energy that everyone pours into the show – including that of the viewers – is tested to the limit in a nail-biting finale. But who knows if the ideal coupling on paper will lead to true love, and an enduring relationship? Or is the last woman standing really after the man of her dreams, or just the massive cash injection that winning will undoubtedly bring? The course of true love runs deep... but not on this show.

Big Brother

One of the most successful 24-hour-surveillance reality TV shows of all time... or a sign of society's complete breakdown with a collection of freaks living in a high-tech prison producing the worst example of junk TV known to man? You decide.

Survivor

As the name suggests, this sophisticated, tropical island game show is all about survival – survival on the show itself, and survival in the extreme environments the contestants find themselves in, which have, over time, become increasingly harsh.

Abandoned in some of the most unforgiving places on earth, the rules are simple: 16 or so 'average' people are divided into teams, and participate in extreme challenges. Every three days, the losing tribe must trek to Tribal Council to vote out one of their own. Eventually, it becomes an individual contest, with each man or woman using whatever skills they have to complete the tasks, and win immunity from eviction, or influence their fellow contestants subtly to gain favour, and so avoid being voted out.

However, players must be careful about who and how they send each other packing – a jury of evictees is then formed, and each week they return to watch the Tribal Council ceremony. At the end of the game, they vote for their favoured winner, who walks off with a cool $1 million. After all that, the million dollars will probably just about cover the therapy the winner will require once they get back to civilisation.

Wife Swap

It does what it says on the tin – families swap their wives for a couple of weeks, causing mayhem, soul searching and often some very entertaining arguments when the two wives eventually meet at the end of the show. Increasingly, producers have endeavoured to swap individuals who lead diametrically opposed lives – a black, vegan, homosexual yoga teacher might swap lifestyles with a fast-food-loving member of the BNP, for example, with hilarious consequences. Again, the only winners seem to be the therapists who will undoubtedly have to pick up the pieces once the show's over.

The Biggest Loser

The biggest winner in this show is the thinnest loser – the person who manages to lose the greatest proportion of their body weight over the course of the programme. In the first series of the show, the winning contestant, Ryan, managed to lose 55 per cent of his body weight, shedding a staggering 7 ? stone. The prize was a year's free delivery of Domino's pizza and a visit to the Hershey Bar factory.

Only joking! He won $250,000 and, more importantly, a future that doesn't involve gasping for air every time he waddles to the fridge.

Celebrity Duets

Well, what do you know, another reality show produced by Simon Cowell. *Celebrity Duets* takes established singing stars and pairs them with celebrities who are normally outside the music industry. The show follows the professional singers as they instruct their celebrity partners, choose songs and perform duets in front of a panel of judges and a live studio audience. Viewers vote on their favourites, and contestants compete for charity... and one tiny consideration is the raising of a public image, or rekindling failing careers. Thank God for celebrity reality TV – without it, Great Britain might have lost the towering talents of Michael Barrymore, Anthea Turner and Les Dennis. Phew!

The Contender

Cross the world of boxing with *The Apprentice* and *Survivor*, and what do you get? *The Contender*. There probably weren't many production meetings to come up with this one, particularly as the producers are linked to other reality TV shows anyway. Essentially, it's a competitive search for the next boxing superstar.

For a gruelling 16 episodes, aspiring boxers slug it out in training camps, specially staged bouts and a Fight of the Week, in which the loser is dumped from the show. It promises blood, sweat and tears, and lots of grunting hunks slugging it out *mano a mano* in the desperate hope of a better future. Oh, and $1 million. Real human drama served up as homespun entertainment, and all accessible in the privacy of your own front room. Fantastic!

Dancing with the Stars

Titled *Strictly Come Dancing* in the UK, *Dancing with the Stars* pairs up celebrities with professional ballroom dance partners in an intense competition – live – in front of a studio audience and the nation. The pairs are then judged by a panel of professional experts as well as by the viewers at home. One team is eliminated each week, and the sound of gnashing teeth, ripping Spandex and wailing divas has become a feature of the show. Of course, that applies to the judges and contestants alike, and particularly the professional dancers, who have never had it so good in terms of televised coverage, and who are fast becoming household names in their own right. For them, the bitterest pill to swallow is being paired with a no-hoper – an elephantine, octogenarian comedian with a hip replacement – and bang goes their chance of staying in the competition long enough to wow the general public, and perhaps be offered a season at a regional theatre in a stage spin-off of the show.

The other significant element to the show for the viewers is keeping one's jaw from hitting the carpet when the dazzling, sequin-covered whirling dervishes eventually shimmy on to the dance floor. Viewers have been known to lunge for the remote and adjust their colour tuning for fear of having their retinas frazzled irreparably.

Extreme Makeover

The magic of *Extreme Makeover* is simple – take the ugliest, most repulsive members of the human race, expose them to the 'Extreme Team', an army of 'the nation's top plastic surgeons, eye surgeons and cosmetic dentists, along with a talented team of hair and makeup artists, stylists, and personal trainers', and completely transform them, Cinderella-style, to something vaguely acceptable by modern society's standards. Oh, and try to make them well-adjusted, rounded individuals who are confident, assertive and content with themselves as well. And all in a one-hour episode. Thank God for television, and the positive life changes it can bring lucky victims.

Hell's Kitchen

Or to put it another way, world-renowned chef Gordon Ramsay tries to conquer America by screaming foul-mouthed abuse at lambs to the slaughter who desperately try to fulfil the demands of a Michelin kitchen when most of them haven't cooked much more than toast. And they're the ones who end up being toast when Gordon sinks his teeth into them. There would be no programme if they were any good, so the producers must have scoured the States for 'chefs' who don't know one end of a courgette from the other.

Laguna Beach

Want to watch how the other half live? Spoilt, rich and with hormones zinging about at record levels, *Laguna Beach* documents the activities of eight gorgeous teenagers, who reside in one of the most beautiful and privileged beachside communities in the world. But the idyllic setting, and the model looks can't hide what's lurking just beneath the surface – human nature. Real life has a habit of intervening, so the tensions, bitching, jealousies, getting together and splitting up of teenage life are all there to be seen, digested, talked about and then forgotten, in time for the next episode. Welcome to a little slice of heaven... or is it hell?

Last Comic Standing

Much like *Pop Idol* for stand-up comedians, the show is a talent search for the best professional and nonprofessional stand-up comedians. Once the selection process is narrowed to ten competitors, the show follows the contestants as they live together and compete for an exclusive contract with NBC. Perhaps the most interesting thing about this show is just how dull comics can be when they aren't on stage... and how desperate some can be to outdo their colleagues. A man and his jokes – perhaps the deadliest combination in light entertainment.

Project Runway

With Heidi Klum as one of the celebrity judges, viewers are guaranteed. Let's face it, she could just sit there for half an hour doing her nails, and she'd get a pretty sizeable audience. But *Project Runway* does a great deal more than that – it's a behind-the-scenes documentary series and competition set in the fashion industry, in which up-and-coming designers compete in weekly challenges. Eventually, they are given all the resources of a top designer to prepare for a high-profile show. Armed with scissors, taffeta and egos the size of a small country, the designers on this show are not to be messed with, or queeny tantrums are a very real possibility. You have been warned.

The Real World

The Real World was the first reality show on TV, being aired in its original format in 1992. It is still on the air, and has remained the forerunner of a genre that has been copied time and again by other networks around the world.

MTV originally wanted to make a soap, but the budget prohibited that, so some bright spark wondered if they could ditch the actors, script, designers, set builders… and the result was *The Real World*, set in the New York neighbourhood of SoHo, Manhattan, where seven people who had never met before had to share a house, and each other's lives, in front of a battery of television cameras.

Just how 'real' this show actually is, we'll never know. Editorial decisions are bound to affect the impression the viewer gets of events or individuals, but it is as close to reality as a house full of carefully selected roommates in a constantly monitored environment can be.

Rock Star

Rock Star combines the world of rock 'n' roll with an unscripted reality series. The 15 performers live together in a Hollywood Hills home, face tough competitions and a weekly elimination. The prize? The coveted lead singer spot of a popular rock band, going off on a world tour and taking part in the group's new album. Of course, they have to be up for the sex and drugs as well – just coping with the rock 'n' roll will not cut the mustard.

The Simple Life

Utterly spoiled, fabulously wealthy and too stupid to realise that the world wants to laugh *at* you, not *with*

you? Then you must be Paris Hilton and Nicole Richie, stars of *The Simple Life*.

The basic format of the show sees these spoilt little rich girls having to slum it among the middle classes and – worse still – actually spending time with the working classes as well! Flipping burgers, milking cows… the sound of nail technicians – and cows – gasping in horror could be heard across the States.

Paris might not realise just what compulsive viewing she makes, but she most certainly is acutely aware of just how lucky she's been: 'Every woman should have four pets in her life – a mink in her closet, a jaguar in her garage, a tiger in her bed, and a jackass who pays for everything.'

Who's the sucker? The burger joint owner who sees his profits going up in smoke, or the viewer who can't help turn on their telly to make them such stars?

So You Think You Can Dance

How much more of this can you take? The merry-go-round of reality shows that differ minutely from each other seems to turn without any sign of the ride stopping. In this show, contestants perform a particular style of dance each week with a partner. The audience votes for their favourite couple – again providing massive profits for the TV company and producers – and one unlucky pair is kicked off the show. Or are they the lucky ones?

Starting Over

Starting Over is a daytime reality show from the creators of *The Real World* which follows six women from all walks of life who overcome issues that have troubled them for years. Life coaches take them through the various activities, exercises and soul-searching that they hope will lead them to more fulfilling, contented lives. Although why they felt the need to go on television and expose their foibles to the nation remains a mystery.

The Surreal Life

Once, they were superstars... then they disappeared into obscurity... and now they're shoved back in the spotlight as they share a home and a series of outrageous and life-changing events for ten days and nights that producers would like everyone to regard as 'surreal', although anyone with half a brain cell would actually regard as 'completely nuts'.

The recipe for *The Surreal Life* is simple: take six larger-than-life, former celebrities from every discipline and throw them together under pressure. Trapped in this celebrity Broadmoor, they must either get on with each other – cleaning, cooking, shopping and evacuating their bowels – or kill each other. Friendships and enmities are dutifully recorded and piped out to millions of interested viewers.

Treasure Hunters

Treasure Hunters is an adventure quest series with multi-player teams given the challenge of searching around the world for clues that will lead to hidden treasure. It's a little like the classic film *It's a Mad Mad, Mad, Mad World*, but with none of the jokes.

BEST BRITISH REALITY TV COMEBACKS

PETER ANDRE

A one-hit wonder who fiddled with his knobs as a 'record producer' for years, then found himself engulfed by the human bouncy castle that is Jordan. A comeback legend.

JOE PASQUALE

The helium-fuelled funny-man rediscovered a whole new audience on *I'm a Celebrity*…and was crowned King of the Jungle when everyone wanted to cuddle him for being lovely. Who says the nice guys nice don't win? He's now cashing in on one-man shows touring around the country.

TONY BLACKBURN

Never far away from the spotlight, Tony was hovering on the fringes of celebrity for years, until the jungle propelled him back into the public consciousness. It had as much to do with him being a decent chap, and rather ancient, as it did with the speculation over whether he wears a nylon toupée. No one could prove it either way, so the tittle-tattle raged on in the tabloids, and Tony – awful jokes and all – won a warm place in everyone's hearts.

CLAIRE SWEENEY

Claire 'Jazz Hands' Sweeney became a new force to be reckoned with when she appeared on Celebrity Big Brother. At the time, viewers turned to one another and said, 'I know the fat one, the bald one, and the one who's carrying around half of Silicon Valley, but who's *she*?' Claire went from zero to vaguely recognisable, and has now become established as a major musical theatre star. Not bad for a bit-part actor in *Brookside*.

KERRY KATONA

Yet another Queen of the Jungle – that Australian backdrop has a lot to answer for. Kerry slummed it, screamed and cried her way through her ordeal, and viewers were gripped by her 'ordinary lass' image and her fear of anything that crawled, squeaked or slithered. And that was just her fellow contestants.

Since her win, Kerry has appeared on our screens

about 47 times a day, and is now even more over-exposed than Carol Vorderman. Her blokes, kids, shopping habits, sneezes, outfits and nightclub antics are all chronicled in every gossip magazine, and she's fronting ads for various companies on TV and in the press. Just shows you how a nibble on a kangaroo's testicle can set you up for life.

LES DENNIS

Most of the British population could be forgiven for forgetting that he ever existed. He was the partner of Dustin Gee, and had his own TV show, but as the appeal of 'northern' comedy formats and variety entertainment waned, so did his popularity. He'd been in the doldrums for ages, although his tempestuous marriage to Amanda Holden kept him hovering around the tabloids like a singed moth.

Celebrity Big Brother changed all that, and he is now used in TV sitcoms and dramas in cameo roles, and has won some sympathy for his readiness to send himself up. A good job, really, because there are plenty of others who would happily do the job for him.

TOP REALITY TV EARNERS

In Britain, the popularity of reality TV shows no sign of abating. Neither does the public's desire to appear on them. The so called celebs from the Z-list who clamour to appear can obviously command more money than Joe Public. Michael Barrymore's fee for appearing on *Big Brother* was reputed to have been around £150,000. However, thousands of wannabes are queuing up for their chance in the TV spotlight, and to dip into the apparently bottomless barrel of gold.

Perform well and you get poached for another show – and the spin-off earnings can soon start to roll in. With both Jade and Jodie Marsh in our top ten proves that it is easier to make a million from reality TV than winning the lottery.

THE TOP TEN BRITISH REALITY TV CELEBS

1: JORDAN – £5 MILLION

Appearances: *Selling Sex; Jordan: You Don't Even Know Me; I'm a Celebrity, Get Me out of Here!; When Jordan Met Peter; Jordan and Peter Laid Bare; Jordan and Peter Get Married.*

The glamour model started off with *Selling Sex* in 2000 but bigger earners were shows about herself such as *Jordan: You Don't Even Know Me.* When she lured and bagged Peter Andre in *I'm a Celebrity...* she doubled her earnings. And for a one-hit wonder pop star 15 years ago, he didn't do too badly either. ITV's *When Jordan Met Peter* and *Jordan and Peter Laid Bare* earned her a million, as book sales and mag deals augmented her income.

Low point: Chomping on a fish eye in the jungle.

2: JADE GOODY – £3.3 MILLION

Appearances: *Big Brother 3*; *Back to Reality*; *What Jade Did Next*; *Jade's Salon*; *Celebrity Driving School*; *Hell's Kitchen*; *Celebrity Wife Swap*.

The apparently mega-thick guttermouth who came fourth in *Big Brother 3* has made a very astute mountain of cash from living her life in front of the cameras. The busy young entrepreneur has since appeared in several shows showcasing her... well... 'talent' is not the word, but she's undoubtedly got something that producers, TV execs and the public find appealing enough to want to have in their front rooms.

Low point: Showing the nation her 'kebab' and her 'minging' verruca.

3: REBECCA LOOS – £1.5 MILLION

Appearances: *The Farm*; *Extreme Celebrity Detox*; *Love Island*; *The X Factor: Battle of the Stars*.

Can a celebrity shag ever have produced so much for so little? The woman who made her name by allegedly

bedding Becks proved where there's muck there's brass on *The Farm* for Channel Five. Channel 4's *Extreme Celebrity Detox* was another shot in the arm and *Love Island* continued her romance with the small screen which saw her hitting all the wrong notes on *The X Factor: Battle of the Stars*.

Low point: Collecting semen from a pig on *The Farm*. The worst aspect was the humiliation of having to touch something really disgusting...

4: JODIE MARSH – £1.5 MILLION

Appearances: *Essex Wives*; *The Games*; *Celebrities Under Pressure*; *Back to Reality*; *Trust Me: I'm a Holiday Rep*; *Celebrity Big Brother*.

The 32FF glamour model kicked off her TV career with *Essex Wives* in 2002. Then came *The Games*, *Celebrities Under Pressure*, *Back to Reality*, *Trust Me: I'm a Holiday Rep* and *Celebrity Big Brother*, for which she was reportedly paid £30,000. Her autobiography, *Keeping It Real*, earned her £1 million.

Low point: Being savaged by Michael Barrymore on *Celebrity Big Brother*.

5: SOPHIE ANDERTON – £220,000

Appearances: *Cold Turkey*; *I'm a Celebrity…*; *Love Island*.

When she appeared on *Love Island*, bra model Sophie was reportedly getting the highest fee – £70,000-£35,000 for each boob. Her stock shot up after *I'm a Celebrity...* where she earned £50,000 for snacking on kangaroo testicles. Her bank balance was already boosted by shows such as *Cold Turkey* when she quit smoking with Tara Palmer-Tomkinson. Strange that, as several celebrities have been quoted as saying that Tara Palmer-Tomkinson had driven them to fags in the first place.

Low point: The only girl not picked as a guy's favourite in *Love Island* – even after Alicia Douvall.

6: VICTORIA HERVEY – £100,000

Appearances: *Love Island*; *The Farm*; *Drop the Celebrity*.

'It' girl Victoria hasn't been tempted to get a proper job, despite her dismal performances as a rent-a-celeb on reality TV. So far, she has 'starred' in *The Farm*, *Drop the Celebrity* and *Love Island*, and the sooner reality television disappears from our screens, the sooner Victoria will have to experience the real meaning of the word 'reality', and get a job like the rest of the population. Low point: Sunbathing naked on *Love Island* in a shameless attempt to win votes, and being the first celebrity voted out of *The Farm*.

7: JAMES HEWITT – £91,000

Appearances: *Under Hypnosis*; *The X Factor: Battle of the Stars*; *Celebrity Wrestling*; *Fool around with My Girlfriend*.

How the mighty have fallen! Having charmed, seduced and then bedded – allegedly – the Princess of Wales, the former cavalry officer has gone from strength to strength, with appearances on some of Britain's trashiest reality shows. Much like Neil and Christine Hamilton and Paul Burrell, Diana's former butler, reality television has kept the wolf from the door for several years now.

Earnings reputedly range from £1,000 for *James Hewitt: Under Hypnosis*, to £30,000 for *The X Factor: Battle of the Stars*. Other 'highlights' include *Fool around with My Girlfriend* and *Celebrity Wrestling*. Unfortunately, he survived the latter, and lives to appear on yet more reality shows coming to a television near you.

Low point: Being regressed back to the time he first slept with Princess Diana. Some have commented that perhaps a bigger challenge would have been regressing him back to a time when he was a decent human being.

8: JEFF BRAZIER – £65,000

Appearances: *Shipwrecked II*; *Back to Reality*; *I'm Famous and Frightened!*; *The Farm*; *Celebrity Wrestling*; *Celebrity Wife Swap*.

When you've had intimate knowledge of Jade Goody's

kebab, and you've been on the receiving end of her Mersey Tunnel-sized mouth, haven't you suffered enough? Jeff – Jade's ex – surely must feel he's been catapulted from the frying pan into the fire, despite some decent money for his reality exploits. His agent has a lot to answer for.

Having done nothing other than play second fiddle to the thickest girl in Britain, according to the tabloids, he fell for the lucrative allure of shows like *Shipwrecked II* and *Back to Reality*. Then came *I'm Famous and Frightened!*, *The Farm* and *Celebrity Wrestling*. His fees – from £3,000 to £8,000 – are paltry compared to Jade's, but he's now a TV presenter. And he can probably always get a freebie back, sack and crack wax in Jade's salon.

Low point: Talking to *Who Wants to Be a Millionaire*'s Diana Ingram while clubbing on *Celebrity Wife Swap*. And having the memories of a naked Jade in his head.

9: SHANE LYNCH – £35,000

Appearances: *The Games*; *Love Island*; *The Match*; *Celebrity Fear Factor*.

When half the population reads that Shane Lynch is on a reality show, you know you're in trouble when most of them go, 'Who?' He may have been in Boyzone several decades ago – at least it seems like that – but his inclusion as a celebrity brings new meaning to the phrase 'scraping the barrel'.

Having been bombarded with knickers flung by adoring fans, to slumming it on *Celebrity Fear Factor*, Shane has fallen an awful long way... and then there's *Love Island*, surely the lowest point of any Z-list celeb's career. Admittedly, he has softened the blow by pocketing decent earnings from *Celebrity Fear Factor*, £26,000 for *Love Island* and he did his bit for charity in *The Games* and *The Match*.

Low point: Bursting into tears when his Boyzone band mates supported him during *The Games*.

10: RICARDO RIBEIRO – £30,000

Appearances: *The Salon; Back to Reality; Drop the Celebrity; I'm Famous and Frightened!; Cosmetic Surgery... Live.*

You could be forgiven for wondering who on earth Ricardo is. The camp crimper stunned audiences when he first appeared in Channel 4's *The Salon* in 2003, and then he shocked a nation again when he agreed to a bum lift on *Cosmetic Surgery... Live.* He even managed to land a lucrative contract to front shampoo ads. His newly chiselled buttocks presumably had nothing to do with his casting, but someone, somewhere, clearly feels that they might help to sell more shampoo.

Low point: Resigning from *The Salon*.

7
The A to Z of Celebrity Status

Your essential guide to the world of celebrity

A – ADDICTIONS

Every celebrity has one, whether it's shoes, sex or drugs… or just the desperation of maintaining a celebrity lifestyle. Pete Doherty is famous for his – and let's be honest, would we be as interested in him if he was clean living? We might notice his music more, but he wouldn't make as many headlines.

Ivana Trump is famous for divorcing Donald and buying shoes with her multimillion pound settlement. And then there's Michael Douglas, who checked into rehab for a reported 'sex addiction'. You have to wonder what the therapy's like. Going 'cold turkey' from that particular condition conjures up all sorts of images, and perhaps marrying Catherine Zeta-Jones wasn't the wisest of moves if you're serious about weaning yourself off all bedroom activity for a while.

B – BREASTS

Think very carefully about what you have or haven't got. Men – get rid of them! Nobody likes man-boobs, and no one is going to believe you when you say that you've come out in sympathy with your pregnant wife.

Ladies – it's all about balance. Not whether you can balance a cup of coffee on them, but whether they're too big or too small. Do they suit you? Is your rack impressive enough or does it look like a bag of watermelons on the verge of exploding? And what will a retouching artist have to do to your chest to get the requisite attention? But beware! While you may yearn for fully rounded, sit-up-and-beg, come-to-momma breasts that offer a tantalising glimpse of the sexy woman within – remember, that may be the only part of you that anyone remembers, or looks forward to seeing. Don't be overshadowed by your breasts! Unless you're Ronnie Corbett out for an evening with the missus.

C – CELEBRITY

Nirvana... your ultimate goal! The iconic status attributed to people who are genuinely famous, and many more who really aren't. But they think they are.

Celebrity is not restricted to the likes of mega-rich vintage Hollywood legends. For every Brad Pitt and Madonna, there are many others who will turn up to the opening of an envelope for the promise of a couple of quid and a meat pie.

OK! Sold more copies with Jade Goody on the cover than any other edition, including Posh 'n' Becks' wedding. And the great thing is – we can all achieve 'celebrity'; as reality TV proliferates, so do our chances of tasting a bit of the high life.

D – DOGS

Get one! The smaller the better – and you can combine a love of shopping with a need to find an accessory for your pampered pooch – the latest designer, diamond-encrusted winter jacket is a must have.

Paris Hilton has several tiny dogs. They all have ridiculous names like Tinkerbell and Totty. Even Simon Cowell was rumoured to have owned a poodle called Prancer.

Another essential doggy trait that celebrities must master is kissing their dogs, and letting their canine chums slaver drool all over them, particularly in the dog-world equivalent of a snog. Let your pet run its smelly wet tongue all over your face and mouth, and, like Sharon Osbourne, laugh and consider it cute, rather than hurling the dog across the room in disgust and running for the nearest bottle of Dettol.

E – EATING

Claim you love eating. Claim you love your curvaceous, hour-glass figure – then stop eating immediately and lose six stone by the end of the week. Popping off to the loo at regular intervals and coming out while dabbing at your lips will also guarantee the right sort of attention, and a little sympathy. If you can add the fragrant whiff of extreme flatulence, suggesting that you might be on a very specialist diet – tofu and beetroot, for example – then you'll keep people guessing for ages. You might also end up with a very lucrative endorsement of all beetroot-related products. Absolute heaven!

F – FASHION

You have to come up with your own thing and you're guaranteed column inches. If someone had told David Beckham ten years ago that putting on a sarong would propel him to fashion-icon status, he might have strung a whole sentence together in shock.

Sienna Miller kick-started the 'Boho Chic' movement; Sarah Jessica Parker made Manolo Blahniks our footwear fantasy and Jodie Marsh taught us that belts are no substitute for a bra. Although whether Jordan's decision to rein in her bazookas with two small hammocks from Millett's was ill advised, remains to be seen.

G – GAY

It's worth considering if you're not. The day after Will Young won *Pop Idol*, he came out. Genius! Now all those girlies who voted for him couldn't have his babies, but they were all too deeply in love with him to stop adoring him. So Will inadvertently turned his fans into fag hags and attracted a whole other crowd – being in the pink certainly has its advantages. And even better, if you haven't declared your particular interest, but there's wild speculation over it, then you've really made it. Robbie Williams still has a whiff of sexual uncertainty surrounding him, appealing to everyone and anyone, and George Michael in his early days attracted a great deal of attention, speculation and finger pointing. It certainly did nothing to harm his record sales, or his 'Is he, isn't he?' image.

Of course, all sense of 'mystery' was blown away when he was caught cottaging by an off-duty copper, but even here the elements of sleaze, sex, homosexuality, criminality, danger... all combine to make him even more of a talking point – and a hot-property, A-list celeb.

Some celebs have even cottoned on to the fact that they're clearly too safe – being a boring, run-of-the-mill heterosexual doesn't do much to boost flagging sales, or get you column inches. So Madonna snogged Britney in her video, and on stage, and the tabloids had a field day. Keep them guessing, or if you're Elton John, just be as wildly camp as possible. If there's anyone who's managed successfully to tie his sexuality inextricably to his work and image, then it's her... I mean, him.

H – HAIR

Remember the 'Rachel'? It was the only choice for young ladies while *Friends* was on TV the first time round. Around that time, you could walk into a salon and ask for a haircut by name of a TV character. For lads, it was the 'Gazza', and for others, the 'Beckham', although there have been so many styles of Beckham over the last few years that anyone trying to keep up would probably have the look of a dog with mange.

Elton John has challenged receding hairlines by having 'plugs'. When he first did it we were all horrified, but now it's all forgotten. Bruce Willis in *Pulp Fiction* and Freddie Ljungberg have mastered the 'close shave so you'll never know if I'm balding' look perfectly. When Victoria Beckham gets her locks trimmed or extended, it's front page news.

Don't underestimate the power of your follicles – hair today, celeb tomorrow.

I – INVENTIVE

Don't be afraid to create situations and opportunities for yourself. For example, picking a fight with someone in a wine bar is perfect, or nudging them off the pavement outside Madame Jojo's would definitely qualify for instant attention from the paps. Better still, if you're Charlotte Church, try going out and *not* drinking, smoking or retching into a gutter by the side of the road. Now *that* would really shock people.

J – JEALOUS

It's OK to be jealous, but use your little green monsters effectively by starting a loud tabloid bitching session. Jodie Marsh and Jordan have been banging away at each other for years… and who cares who's winning. It keeps them in the papers, and serves each other's purpose. We love all that, so keep at it. Unfortunately, neither of them have been prepared to appear on *Celebrity Mud Wrestling* yet, but they'd be guaranteed a massive audience if they ever agreed to it.

K – KICKS

You may like to reconsider how you get them – and then try to keep them quiet if you persist. For example, how can we ever think of Jamie Theakston as clean cut, knowing that he reportedly had a steamy encounter with a lady of the night?

Chaps, most prostitutes have the editor of the *News of the World* on speed dial – if you're famous, you'll be caught out, quicker than you can say, 'What could you do for £50?' Hugh Grant made the biggest blunder of all in that department, although you might say now that it has done his career the world of good. That element of naughty, edgy cad, which was so lacking in his early career, is now very much a part of his image, and might stand him in good stead for years to come.

Weigh up the pros and cons against an endless world of tabloid coverage... it's your call... and there's nothing quite like a good old-fashioned call girl to stiffen up a limp career.

L – LABELS

Wear them sparingly – no Burberry overload, daaahling – or you could end up looking like Coleen McLoughlin, Wayne Rooney's girlfriend. If you want to look like the Queen of Chavs, then go for it.

An ultimate goal of any aspiring celebrity is to be a designer's muse. Posh is Roberto Carvelli's... and then you can encourage all of your friends to wear their couture frocks. Kate Moss can launch a designer's career by wearing one of their creations, but even the great modern style icons mix and match designer and high street – so Top Shop is still just about acceptable – as long as their gear is offset with £50,000 diamond studs. Remember, it's easy to look cheap, but looking like a celebrity who *wants* to look cheap, but looks cool, takes a lot of know-how, and a massive ego.

M – MUSIC

Never say never... get some singing lessons as there's a load of money to be made by correctly placed novelty singles. The Cheeky Girls (although you may be aiming

 at greater things) can keep themselves in matching minis for ever because of their ridiculous act, which consists of tiny little belt-skirts and lots of arse slapping. There's a fine line between cutesy fun and really irritating – so far, the British public have failed to register just how dreadful the Cheekies are, but it's surely a matter of time.

Chico, an ex-stripping goat herder, rode his luck for several weeks on *The X Factor*, and proved that waggling your hips and making your pecs dance impresses more people than being able to sing in tune. He makes a very good living from repeating the phrase that makes you want to pull out your own fingernails in distress – 'It's Chico time!' Perhaps another sign of his waning popularity is being asked to perform at a bash for another D-lister – Anthea Turner – who was arranging a ball for friends and business pals. Presumably, she didn't like them much.

N – NEPOTISM

Use your family now while you can. Any long-lost second cousin twice removed, or a step-grandmother whom might have a link to a TV producer… use them all, and use them quickly, before they use you to earn a few quid selling lurid tales of your sexual inadequacy to the tabloids.

If great uncle Jack used to go to school with someone famous, encourage him on to Friends

Reunited to rekindle their lost relationship. You must be ruthless and focused and, if you want it badly enough, you'll have no hesitation in selling your granny for a few more minutes in the limelight.

O – ONE NAME

You can gauge your celebrity status by your surname, and whether it's used or not. Your ultimate goal is to be known solely by your first name – Kylie, Madonna, Chantelle, Jade, Jordan, Coleen... they're all up there with the best of them, and you can add Sting, Bono and Shergar to that list as well.

P – PARTNER

Make your choice well. If you embark on your journey to fame then you need to ditch any dead wood, but make sure to end it well to prevent any possible kiss and tells later on.

For the girls, in an ideal world you'd date a footballer or a convicted criminal/junkie/sex addict. It makes interesting copy and will either make you into a glamour puss or sassy rock chick. At this stage, non-celebs would be a no-no.

Boys – go for a page three model/glamour girl/promotions girl/former lap dancer. If someone looks good on your arm, it instantly boosts your street cred and obvious pulling power, making you instantly interesting to other women; you can upgrade your model later.

A warning , though, if you happen to be a Liverpudlian billionaire, and you were part of one of the most famous bands in the world – don't mess with anyone who might end up walking off with half your fortune. It's great when things are rosy, but when the relationship sours, you'll be regretting having dabbled with a bit of lucky Heather.

Q – QUEER NATION

British people love an underdog and are willing to root for anybody. We're very tolerant but very judgemental. Who would have thought that the nation would take to its bosom a slightly odd musician with mascara who suffers from Tourette's syndrome? But for the summer of 2006, twitching and involuntary swearing became adorable.

The great British public is an unpredictable creature… it re-elected Tony Blair, it has chuckled at John Prescott's libido and his secretarial fumblings, and chose to jeer and then cheer a lanky beanpole – Peter Crouch – who looks like the 3D version of Plug from the *Beano*, who ended up as a first-choice striker for the England football team while all the others fell apart, blew up or self-destructed.

It doesn't make sense who they take to their hearts – so there's every chance it could be you.

R – RELIGION

Make one up, join one, find the most obscure world religion you can and wear it on your sleeve! Had the majority of the population heard of Kabbalah or Scientology before Madge or Tom Cruise? Choose wisely – try to avoid the ones that involve ritual sacrifice or drinking rat poison. Making it as a celebrity generally involves remaining alive, so joining a cult is probably best avoided.

S – STALKERS AND STARKERS

A nasty by-product of fame – but only the really desirable and famous get stalked, so you may have to pay a unemployed school friend to do the honours until some lonely weirdo becomes infatuated and does it for nothing.

S can also be for 'starkers' – there's nothing quite like a bit of exposed flesh to get the tabloids' pulses racing, and your profile leaping up several notches. A boob popping out here, a flash of a kebab there... or an 'outrageous' exposé by a tabloid of you sunbathing naked on a beach in St Tropez. Amazing how the paps got such great shots, and knew exactly where you'd be, eh? Good work – you're definitely getting the hang of this.

T – TROUBLE

If you want to be rebellious and fabulous then choose the kind of trouble you get into carefully. Cheryl Tweedy had an incident in a nightclub and came out of it hard as nails, despite the fact that she allegedly made racial slurs to provoke

the girl who brought the complaint. That's all forgotten now – all we remember is that Cheryl's a hard bitch who deserves serious 'respeck'.

Pete Doherty is always in trouble, yet he affects a permanent lost schoolboy look which demands forgiveness from some, and mothering from others.

George Michael is teaching us how to stay out of trouble – falling asleep at your steering wheel is bad; flashing at undercover cops is worse and cruising notorious cottaging districts and rummaging in the undergrowth is just plain bonkers.

U – UNDERWEAR

You can flash it or start your own line in it. Let's start with the former. If you had been the bride at the wedding when Liz Hurley wore bejewelled pants, you would have been bloody livid. Liz got snapped and won several pages of tabloid coverage. She's a supreme mistress of monopolising column inches and double-page spreads, and if you've got a body as fabulous as hers, then why wouldn't you wear a few scraps of tissue paper and hold them together with safety pins?

If you design your own range of underwear, then people will associate you with those sexy, silken undergarments and transfer that image to you – unless you're Michelle McManus. Kylie, who spent most of her formative career years wearing little more than pants, has a very successful line of lingerie, as does Caprice! And if you want a little bit of Kylie next to

111

your nether regions, then close your eyes and pull her pants on.

V – VIRGINITY

If you're young enough to get away with it, then claim you're still a virgin. Everyone will be talking about it and speculating whether some great hairy brute has stolen it yet.

Britney is a classic example. We all wanted to believe her when she was prancing about in bunches and school uniforms, but as soon as she started wrapping snakes around her neck it was clear she'd lost it.

The cherry on the cake is to lose your virginity to someone equally famous. Gareth Gates was reputedly taken in hand by Jordan, who proceeded to spill the beans and shoot her mouth off in her book. Poor Gareth didn't come off very well at all.

W – WARDROBE MALFUNCTIONS

A wardrobe malfunction is when a horrendous 'accident' occurs to your clothing, resulting in the exposure of certain parts of your anatomy. Those in the know, though, are fully aware of just how sophisticated a stunt this can be, to make it look like a genuine error. And the bigger the boob... er, mistake... the bigger the coverage.

How to do it? Get Justin Timberlake to whip one of your breasts out on prime-time American TV in front of 20 million people. Or just wear a really badly fitting bra, Judy Finnigan.

This is also achievable on a smaller scale, if you fancy streaking at a major sporting event. The regular offenders have gained some notoriety in the press.

X – THE X FACTOR

There is that indefinable star quality that is referred to as 'it'. You either have 'it' or you don't… but set yourself on the right path and you can almost create it yourself.

In terms of a singing career, if you're serious about it and you can't sing, you will be found out… Milli Vanilli, anyone?

But you don't really need 'it' to be famous any more. As we are all now aware, there are many 'celebs' on our screens who have no obvious talent, who look like the back end of a rhino, and have back ends the size of a rhino, and who no one likes. How they manage to remain in the limelight is a complete mystery, yet they still achieve the impossible. Fair play to them – serious contenders for How the Hell Have You Managed to Stay in the Public Eye When You Have No Talent at All Award.

Y – YES

Say yes to everything that comes your way apart from porn. Even if it's sold to you as a 'glamour job', if you achieve greatness it will still be seen as porn. There's no way you will ever be taken seriously if you've been spotted being taken from behind by a Swedish plumber. Would Dame Judi Dench or Sir Michael Caine have got their gongs if we'd suddenly discovered that they'd appeared in *Look Who's Porking* or *Shaving Private Ryan*? I think not!

Z – Z-LIST CELEBS

Everyone has to start somewhere, but you must not remain at the arse end of the alphabet for long. If all you want to do is make car-crash TV, appear on *Celebrity Big Brother* and cry like a self-pitying hobbit (Barrymore), or agree to a stint on *Love Island*, then go forth and 'zedify'. You're the celebrity equivalent of pond life, and should be treated as such.

But, if you're aiming at the lofty heights of a Jade Goody or a Chantelle, then claim your 15 minutes, grasp it with both clammy hands and if you're a lucky wannabe and you hold on tight, it could last that little bit longer. And if you remember to let a boob pop out, allow you clothes to fall off, roll out of a club drunk, get a chihuahua, become addicted to smack, dabble in gay sex, become a Bhuddist, flash your kebab to the paparazzi and remain a virgin… then you'll probably make it as an A-list celeb.

8

Is It Just Me or Is Everyone Stinking Rich?

The celebrity fragrance hit parade

1: INTIMATELY BECKHAM BY VICTORIA

The official blurb would have us believe that 'the essence' of one of Britain's most celebrated, photographed, criticised and gossiped-about celebrities of the modern era is known only to those who are closest to her. And that lucky recipients of Intimately Beckham will be enveloped with an opulent bouquet of white flowers and 'pure fresh notes of bergamot and rose petals that linger on the skin.'

This contrasts with the image sometimes portrayed in the media which could be expressed as, 'the essence of Victoria... loud, shrill notes and a stick-thin image that lingers long in the memory. It's full of wonder... you can't help wondering why a bloke like David fell for a girl like her.'

2. SHH BY JADE GOODY

Jade's scent was created by legendary French perfumer Robertet, who have chosen 'bergamot and cassis with heart notes of pink pepper, cinnamon, cumin, freesia, jasmine, rose and iris.'

It would be interesting to see how a perfume marketed as, 'New, brash, thick and long-lasting' would fare.

3. LOVELY BY SARAH JESSICA PARKER

The press release for Sarah Jessica Parker Lovely tells us that it is a joy to wear, beginning with 'a truly sparkling and dazzling burst of fresh mandarin, bergamot and radiant rosewood, which mellow to reveal a beautiful veil of lush lavender and crisp apple martini.'

If you can't find a bottle of the stuff at your local department store, why not just nip down the greengrocer's and get yourself some real mandarins and apples. You won't smell as lovely, but at least you'll have something towards your five-a-day.

4. LIVE BY J LO

Driven to fulfill your dreams like Jennifer Lopez? Why not nab yourself the 'vivacious blend of sparkling fruits, sensual flowers, and soft, sexy musk, serene vanilla, and warm woods' of Live by J Lo?

Perhaps a perfume promoted as 'Well-rounded with a lot of cheek' would be more appropriate.

5. CAT DELUXE BY NAOMI CAMPBELL

Naomi, like Jade, plumbed for Robertet for a perfume full 'freesia, cardamom, violet, peony, peach, woods, musk, patchouli and vanilla.'

So even if you're an Anne Widdecombe lookalike, maybe you too could have blokes falling over themselves to have a sniff.

6. SUMMER BY CINDY CRAWFORD

Unsurprisingly, for multimillionaire supermodel, covergirl, Hollywood actress and *Playboy* sexiest star of the twentieth century, 'on some days, everything just seems right. You wake up with a smile – kissed by the summer sun – and you just know this is going to be your day.'

If you're a debt collector in Stoke and don't share Cindy's enviable lifestyle, then a swig of Cindy's perfume might soften the blow.

7. INTIMATELY BECKHAM BY DAVID

David's advert tells of 'a heady mix of energy, vibrancy, comfort and warmth. Magnetic, provocative, cool – yet never aloof, he is aspirational but within reach.'

Presumably he wasn't wearing any during World Cup 1998, Euro 2004 or World Cup 2006…

8. SIMON COWELL MAKES A NASTY SMELL

Simon Cowell has been approached by an American cosmetic giant to put his name to a new range of after shave. He's been offered a vast sum of money to do the deal. Mr Nasty will never smell as sweet ... I know what I'm going to get for Christmas.

9
The Icons

*'A celebrity is a person who works hard all of
their life to become well known, and then wears dark
glasses to avoid being recognised.'*
FRED ALLEN, US RADIO COMEDIAN

In your quest to be famous, you must first study the rise and fall of our current celebrities. What is it that makes them famous and, more importantly, how did they become famous in the first place? Up to this point, we have looked at the plethora of reality TV shows that have become part of our viewing pleasure.

Many of today's celebrity icons have found fame from appearing on these shows – but many who sought fame have not endured. Let's take a closer look at our reality TV winners and losers and explore their 'talents' more closely.

JORDAN, AKA KATIE PRICE
Most famous quote: 'Some people may be famous for creating a pencil sharpener. I'm famous for my tits.'

Jordan has become a household name. In addition to modelling, her first autobiography, *Being Jordan*, sold more than a million copies, and the follow-up, *A Whole New World*, reached Number One in the hardback non-fiction charts, selling over 400,000 copies. She has also signed a £2.8 million deal to design a lingerie range and is working on a line of shoes and a children's book.

Jordan began appearing on Page Three of the *Sun* newspaper at a time when her breasts were simply impressive, rather than the meteor-sized boulders we know and love today. As her career began to blossom, Jordan embarked on several brief relationships with celebrities and sports stars including footballers Teddy Sheringham and Dwight Yorke, and a more serious relationship with the TV Gladiator 'Ace' (Warren Foreman). All of these 'sexploits', which were liberally splashed all over the tabloids, helped her to remain constantly in the public eye.

Despite Jordan's declaration of love for the *Gladiator* star, the relationship didn't last. Jordan subsequently wrote in her first autobiography of Warren's extreme jealousy. It must be tricky being somebody's squeeze while attracting bucketloads of attention from unknown male admirers. An inevitable dilemma if dating a topless model.

Its fair to say that Jordan has made headlines because of her breast size. Just for the record, from the time she first appeared on Page Three her breasts have gone from a size 32A to 34FF. However, the fact remains that she took her chances and was determined to make it to the top. She was also the first Page Three girl to make it on to reality TV. Jordan did everything right. She went out with footballers and pop stars and made sure the paps were on hand to record her every breath... and even her breaths were huge.

Jordan's private life, wild behaviour and outrageous antics – most of which happened in swish nightclubs – have been extensively detailed by the paparazzi. One of her first public relationships was with the pop singer Dane Bowers, of the boyband Another Level. They ended their relationship while she was pregnant by him, leading her to have an abortion. Their on-off relationship was regularly played out in the press and Jordan would often be quoted making derogatory comments about Bowers, including a less than flattering description of his chipolata-sized appendage. Their break-up came just as Bowers was recording a single with ex-Spice Girl Victoria Beckham. So began a long-standing, bitter feud between Jordan and Victoria, which has been played out in the tabloids to this day... and guarantees both of them much-needed column inches.

In 2004, Jordan made the big TV breakthrough that would give her career a huge boost and ensure her celebrity A-list status; her agent put her up for *I'm a Celebrity, Get Me out of Here!* The fact that washed-up 1980s pop singer Peter Andre was also on the show gave Jordan a massive opportunity to bare all –

physically and emotionally – as viewers were treated to the extraordinary sight of celebrities hitting on each other, bitching, flirting, fighting, arguing and then smooching, and eventually – almost but not quite – consummating their new-found 'love'.

The brilliance of this courtship display was that viewers were left wondering whether it was all for real, and what would happen next. *I'm a Celebrity...* resurrected both of their careers, and Jordan's antics in the jungle meant that she was rarely out of the British press at this time. Of particular interest was her revelation that she had embarked on a secret fling with a renowned married footballer behind his wife's back. Two autobiographies down, and she still hasn't revealed the footballer's name. The story sparked a plethora of press speculation.

So what does Jordan herself think about the fame game? She says, 'I like to think that I made it on my own. People helped me – but I still did it on my terms. If you want to stay sane in this business, you have to sometimes say *no* to some ideas. It should always be about what you want for yourself.

'I like money, I admit it, but I would hate to be like Victoria Beckham with all her security issues, and her nanny problems. I'm a mum and I manage to look after my own kids even when I'm working. I don't want to live in cloud cuckooland I want to be *me*. I think fame changes you – but it should not change the way you want to live your life.

'Being a celebrity means you have to spend time with your public because they help pay your bills. I like my privacy but I don't mind talking to my fans. When I wrote my first book, I went all round the country doing book signings. It's all part of the fame game.

'I think some of the new [*Big Brother*-type] celebrities don't get the right advice. They are taken for a quick ride and then dumped. The life of a celeb seems to get shorter and shorter if you don't plan your life out properly. Don't be scared about telling people what *you* want out of it all. Ultimately, it will be you who pays everyone's bill.

'Staying a celebrity means you have to learn how to balance your life. Luckily, Peter knows all about that and is very understanding about my work. When you first start out, relationships are the first thing to suffer. Partners get envious of your lifestyle and expect you to take them to every glitzy party. When you do, they get the arse because you don't have time to talk to them. It's hard – but worth it in the end. I wouldn't change my world, but I've been working at it for a long time now and I know the rules.'

JADE GOODY

Most famous quotes: 'Where is East Angular? Is it abroad?'…'I thought chickens ate cheese'…'I'm not being tictactical in here'…'The Union Jack is for all of us, but the St George is just for London, innit?'…'What's a "sparagus"? Do you grow it?'…'I am intelligent, but I let myself down because I can't speak properly or spell'...'Rio de Janeiro...ain't that a person?'...'They were trying to use me as an escape goat.'

Jade Goody is Britain's first reality TV millionairess. The former dental nurse hit our screens in 2002 in the third series of *Big Brother* and has turned her 15 minutes of fame into well over an hour and built a successful celebrity career. It wasn't long before Jade was the most talked about woman in the country. Several years on, Jade still sells more tabloids and magazines than any reality TV star in history.

She is often held by some as a prime example of the growing cult of celebrity – being made arbitrarily famous by the entertainment industry, and becoming a household name due to constant publicity and exposure in glossy magazines.

Jade's fortune is derived from appearing on other reality shows and almost constantly being featured in celebrity, trivia and gossip-oriented magazines such as *Heat* and *OK!*. She also 'writes' a weekly showbiz column for *Closer* magazine; one can only assume that her spelling is being checked by an army of editors.

Jade is perhaps best known for her ability to make the most of her fame. Since leaving the *Big Brother* house, she has given birth to two children, raising them more or less as a single mother. She has completed a beauty therapy course and subsequently opened her own salon. She has also developed and launched her own perfume which, in recent statistics, is outselling those endorsed by J Lo and David Beckham by four to one. Everyone, it seems, wants a little whiff of Jade about them.

Jade Goody's fame may also be due in part to various quotes portraying her as being extremely uneducated and ignorant, and a symbol of British chav culture. She is considered a representative for the perceived attitudes of the British public towards deliberate apathy, trivia and dumbing down. She came fourth in the 100 Worst Britons poll by Channel 4, and she came first in a poll by Kerrang! Radio of the ten ugliest celebrities in the UK. As one of Britain's mingiest mingers, she's not doing too badly!

On 2 May 2006, Goody published her autobiography, in partnership with HarperCollins Entertainment, titled *Jade: My Autobiography* – not surprisingly, it went to the top of the book charts. Unfortunately, there doesn't appear to be a scratch-and-sniff version available yet.

What makes Jade stand out from the majority of reality TV winners, or losers, is her ability to use the media. Not many people would withstand being called ugly, fat, thick and useless. Jade is a natural winner; she courts the media brilliantly, and has capitalised on being an 'ordinary' girl. One thing standing out is her ambition. Don't for one minute underestimate this girl's love of media attention. In her favour is her constant support of charitable causes. Her work in this sphere is endless and she never turns down an opportunity to help others.

REBECCA LOOS

Most famous quote: 'Through hard work and determination, I have successfully established myself as a versatile and talented presenter and actress.'

Rebecca comes from the 'how to make the best out of working for a celebrity' category. When England football captain David Beckham moved to Real Madrid on a four-year contract on 17 June 2003, he and his family hired Rebecca as a personal assistant. Loos was the only employee in SFX's Madrid office (David's agents) who spoke English and Spanish fluently, so she immediately began showing David the ropes in Madrid.

According to SFX, Beckham and Loos worked closely together both professionally and socially, and Loos claimed that she became an 'alternative wife'. As Victoria wanted to develop her UK music career, and as she was not initially happy in Madrid, she spent much of her time in England. Loos claimed this resulted in Beckham becoming bored, with them spending almost all their time together socially, and she claims this eventually led to a four-month affair. Had she been anything other than discreet and loyal, as a friend and employee, that would have been the end of the matter, so the tabloids reported. But she wasn't, apparently, much to David's embarrassment, and the British public's delight. The sound of choking on Cornflakes could be heard from John O'Groats to Land's End when the alleged affair broke.

One little knock on Max Clifford's door did the rest. Loos sold her story to the *News of the World* in April 2004, explaining that they had had a whirlwind affair that included sexy text messages – which were later published. She added to the intense speculation with 'revelations' about Victoria Beckham and then the announcement of her own bisexuality. The story generated a huge amount of publicity in the tabloid press, and Loos was guaranteed her time in the spotlight. Whatever the truth might have been, one thing was certain – Rebecca Loos was now a bankable commodity, and could command some pretty tidy amounts of cash for appearing on third-rate TV shows.

In October 2004, she appeared on the reality television programme *The Farm*. At one point, she was famously given the task of masturbating a pig and collecting its semen. The pig obliged, after a great deal of grunting and squealing.

The broadcast provoked controversy, attracted complaints, and generated extra publicity for Loos, who made tabloid headlines once again as a result. Sales of bacon also dipped to an all-time low. The incident was viewed by some commentators as a perfect example of the depths to which Z-list celebrities would stoop for public exposure, and the lengths to which the producers of reality television would go to humiliate them in order to satisfy the interests of viewers. The RSPCA weighed in on the controversy, claiming that the incident, and indeed the whole series, was evidence of an unhealthy preoccupation with the sexual aspects of farm animals. More to the point, the pig had to share its sty with Loos for at least 15 minutes. An open-and-shut case of cruelty to animals, if ever there was one, and she was caught red-handed, as well!

In 2005, Loos appeared on the ITV reality show *Celebrity Love Island*, where she sparked up a relationship with the model Calum Best. Their flirtatious dalliance managed to cause a stir in the British tabloids when the pair discarded their microphones and disappeared into the resort's toilets. Classy!

She also starred in *The X Factor: Battle of the Stars* in 2006, singing along with fellow celeb James Hewitt. Their chosen charity for the show was Save the Children. The pair received a hostile response from the audience and abuse from judge Sharon Osbourne. They were voted out in the fourth out of eight shows on 1 June 2006. It was public knowledge that Sharon Osbourne did not like Rebecca and insulted her after one of her performances saying, 'You have nice boobs, lady, but you should wear some knickers to warm up your voice.'

Interestingly, Max Clifford had always wanted to act for David Beckham since he had become an international celebrity. He maintained that David was wide open to potential scandal. Allegedly, it was his wife who always resisted Max becoming their publicist!

JODIE MARSH

Most famous quote: 'I could've been a lawyer... but I've taken the easiest, quickest route to making as much money as I can.'

A former topless model and Page Three girl, Jodie made the breakthrough into TV following a steady stream of tabloid headlines on a string of high-profile relationships, including Fran Cosgrave, male model Calum Best and Labour MP Frank Dobson to name but three!

She has taken part in a variety of reality TV shows, including *Trust Me I'm a Holiday Rep* (with other celebs such as Syd Little), Channel 4's *The Games* and Sky One's *Celebrity Penthouse*. In January 2006, she appeared on *Celebrity Big Brother* in the UK. She quickly caused controversy among the housemates, notably Pete Burns, Michael Barrymore and George Galloway. She was also the first to be booted out of the *Big Brother* house.

Jodie is seen as the ultimate ambitious Essex girl with all the attributes that keep the tabloids begging for more. She also writes a weekly column for *Sneak*, a celebrity gossip magazine. Marsh had surgery on her nose at the age of 15, and rival glamour model Jordan has described her nose as

resembling 'a builder's elbow' and likened her breasts to a spaniel's ears.

She inhabited a twilight world of nightclubs, gossip pages and reality TV shows, swimming in the same murky waters as Abi Titmuss and Calum Best. In fact, Marsh arrived, fame-wise, relatively recently, courtesy of the reality show *Essex Wives*, and has, in the intervening time, projected herself as a rival to the glamour model Jordan, sharing her taste for fake tan, pop-star boyfriends and outfits that are cunningly unable to contain her prized assets. Never were the words, 'Tits and teeth, daaaaahling,' more aptly applied.

Jodie Marsh was just another Jordan wannabe, but her brief turn on *Celebrity Big Brother* proved there's far more to her than that. Jodie has pushed ahead with her career following her appearance in the show. Her autobiography, *Keeping it Real*, was a massive hit and she continues to make tabloid headlines. And, let's face it, as long as you can continue to do that, sooner or later you will be considered for another TV reality show.

SOPHIE ANDERTON

Most famous quote: ' I think the Falkland Islands are in Europe.'

Once again, tabloid headlines had a massive effect on the career of Sophie Anderton. The former Gossard bra model was mauled by the tabloids in 2002 when footballer boyfriend Mark Bosnich was involved in a cocaine scandal. In 2004, following a long battle with drink and drugs, she appeared on *I'm a Celebrity, Get Me Out of Here!*, and the work and the money began to flow again.

In 2006, she had another stab at reality TV with *Love Island* – which saw her 'imagining' herself having a relationship with fellow contestant Shane Lynch. Like Jordan, Sophie Anderton is one of those girls who knows how to court the media. When the work dries up, Sophie hits the town and the tabloids greet her like a long-lost friend.

CLAIRE SWEENEY

Most famous quote: 'Fame's been a long time coming.'

Former *Brookside* actress Sweeney appeared on *Celebrity Big Brother* in 2001 in aid of Comic Relief, and for some reason she became big buddies with past-it TV presenter Anthea Turner. Her appearance on the show upped her media profile, and she exploited that increase in interest by landing a leading role in the musical *Chicago* in London. She won Rear of the Year in 2001, which helped, too. In 2002, she hosted BBC TV's *A Song for Europe* contest.

She has also presented a number of shows, such as *Challenge of a Lifetime* and *60 Minute Makeover*. In 2004, she participated in the first series of the BBC1 pro-celebrity ballroom dancing competition *Strictly Come Dancing*.

On 10 July 2006, Sweeney took over from Sally Ann Triplett in the role of Miss Adelaide in the UK production of *Guys and Dolls* at the Piccadilly Theatre in London's West End for an eight-week run. Sweeney played opposite *Dirty Dancing* legend Patrick Swayze. Unlike some of her fellow celebs, who are famous for doing nothing, Claire has clearly earned her place in the celebrity pantheon.

JAMES HEWITT

Most famous quote: 'I always like to pay my way…'

In her infamous *Panorama* interview, Princess Diana admitted that she had committed adultery with James Hewitt, saying, 'Yes, I adored him…yes, I was in love with him.' And the British public screamed as one: 'WAKE UP AND SMELL THE COFFEE, WOMAN!'

From the moment Diana died, James Hewitt cashed in. A best-selling book telling the story of his affair with Diana kicked off a career that led to numerous lucrative TV appearances, with one of his first being Channel 4's *The Games* in 2003. The same year, James took part in the Channel Five reality TV show *Back to Reality* and eventually won it.

In 2005, he took part in the ITV wrestling competition *Celebrity Wrestling*, and he also appeared in *Heads Up* with Richard Herring to discuss his life, career and his love of poker.

In 2006, he appeared on the BBC show *Top Gear* as

a celebrity guest, achieving a lap time of 1.47.69, although he was not recognised by presenters Jeremy Clarkson and Richard Hammond, who referred to him as 'the well-spoken man'. He was then seen on the Sky One show *Vroom Vroom*, where he accepted the Cat and Mouse Challenge.

In May, Hewitt was a contestant on *The X Factor: Battle of the Stars*, alongside fellow 'celebrity' Rebecca Loos, but was evicted after the final showdown. It was not revealed whether she had approached him backstage with a rubber glove and a specimen bottle.

Love him or hate him, Hewitt cannot lose financially. Given his past, Hewitt will always be in demand by the media. This is kiss and tell at the highest level and the fact remains that he has the celebrity nous – and the rakish charm – to carry it off.

JEFF BRAZIER

Most famous quote: 'I wanted to be famous and I am.'

Jeff Brazier is a shining example of how reality TV can propel a nobody to celebrity status in the time it takes you to switch from Channel 4 to Channel Five.

How? In 2001, Jeff Brazier took part in the Channel 4 reality TV show *Shipwrecked*. With pretty-boy looks and a cheeky on-screen persona, Jeff was soon in demand for a host of other TV opportunities, including *Simply the Best*, *Dirty Laundry* and *Celebrity Wife Swap* with Jade Goody and Charles Ingram. Jade eventually married Jeff after a whirlwind romance of the sort the tabloids love.

In September 2004, Jeff won the Channel Five reality TV show *The Farm*. He also appeared in the Living TV programme *I'm Famous and Frightened!*

With two children from his fling with Jade Goody, Jeff is not shy of doing his fair share of charity work. Along with Jade, he is an active supporter of the NSPCC. His original £65,000 earnings from reality TV have since been eclipsed by the salary he is paid for his new stint as a presenter on *This Morning*.

So what is Jeff's appeal? Well, he's not ugly, and…well…that's about it. He's the human equivalent of muzak in a lift.

LADY VICTORIA HERVEY

Most famous quote: 'I think I'm quite bright really.'

Posh totty, leggy blonde, brain of an amoeba…one of the original 'It' girls, famous for being famous, and dating people like Shane Lynch and David Coulthard.

Victoria, a former Dior model, may not be Britain's most cerebral celeb, and she has had that most bankable of backgrounds – a traumatic upbringing, that has elicited a great deal of sympathy for her before she has even had to open her mouth. Her playboy father became the first English marquess to go to prison for theft, and her half-brother Johnnie, the 7th Marquess, was a ne'er-do-well and drug addict. He was jailed for nine months for smuggling cocaine into Jersey. Victoria's second half-brother, Lord Nicholas Hervey, was a schizophrenic who hanged himself in 1998.

So far, Victoria's reality TV success has only included stints on *The Farm, Drop the Celebrity* and *Love Island*. It is interesting to note she was paid £50,000 for appearing on the show, which is not bad for lying naked on a tropical beach and scratching your bum for a few days. It beats working, anyway.

KATE LAWLER

Most famous quote: 'I do love the attention I've been getting.'

The first female winner of *Big Brother 3* in 2002. Kate went on to work as a DJ on Capital Radio and co-presented the breakfast TV programme *RI:SE*.

She hit the tabloids in 2003 after announcing her engagement to footballer Jonathan Woodgate. In 2005, she was one of the competitors in the ITV show *Celebrity Wrestling*, competing under the name 'The Brawler'. Not one to miss a golden opportunity for exposure, in more ways than one, she hit the tabloids hard with plenty of skimpy bikini-wrestling shots. She now works as a club 'DJ' in Europe and is an occasional columnist for the UK-based celebrity gossip magazines *OK!* and *New*.

As with many reality TV celebs, Lawler has managed to keep herself in the media spotlight through paparazzi shots of her at the beach. In 2006, Ann Summers announced that Lawler would be the company's new model in its lingerie advertisements.

In August 2006, she entered *Love Island 2* as a new arrival, much to the chagrin of Sophie Anderton. Kate finished up as the third girl finalist.

SHANE LYNCH

Most famous quote: 'I've said a lot of stupid things.'

The former Boyzone member has had a good try at reality TV, appearing in *The Games*, *The Match*, *Celebrity Fear Factor* and *Love Island*.

While pocketing only £26,000 from his brief run on *Love Island*, Shane keeps trucking along. He's got the ability and the fan base to go the whole way, but Shane has a small attention span and gets bored easily. He is now a born-again Christian. He needs a new challenge (or a Boyzone reunion tour) to get back on track. Shane has never really got over the loss of being in a famous boyband and all the security that goes with it. And he now has to buy all his own hair gel. Shame, Shane!

RICARDO RIBEIRO

Most famous quote: 'Oh dear, I'm really scared.'

Ricardo is a camp Brazilian celebrity hairdresser, who first became famous on British television after appearing in *The Salon*. He then went on to be a contestant on such programmes as *The Weakest Link*,

Drop the Celebrity, Back to Reality, and *I'm Famous and Frightened!* for Living TV in which he was runner-up.

Ricardo's claim to fame is his campness. The Brits have always loved plenty of queeny mincing around, from Kenneth Williams on *Round the Horn,* to John Inman and Larry Grayson, to Graham Norton and Julian Clary. For Ricardo, it meant that there was life after *The Salon* and he has managed to squeeze every ounce of exposure out of a very mundane appeal. Unfortunately for him, there seem to be too few skeletons in his closet to keep the tabloids interested – he really needs to end up with a rent boy, or go out with a footballer...or even worse, confess to being heterosexual. Now *that* would get the fur flying!

PETE BENNETT

Most famous quote: 'Wankers!'

Tourette's sufferer Pete Bennett won the seventh series of *Big Brother* hands down. His characteristic so-called 'phonic tic' is a loud shout of 'Wankers'. Pete entered the *Big Brother* house after supposedly experiencing a premonition. According to Pete, a friend of his who died appeared before him in a vision, and told him that in order to leave hell and discover himself again, he needed to enter *Big Brother* and win. So far so good then.

Pete was the second entrant into the *Big Brother* house, and made an immediate impression as he tumbled down the stairs. Pete had many admirers in

Britain's most high-tech asylum, but it was blonde moaner Nikki Grahame whom he eventually fell for.

After pocketing his £100,000 prize, Pete is hoping to further his pop career and has been reputedly writing songs with Guy Chambers. His first single will probably be called 'Wankers!'

NIKKI GRAHAME

Most famous quote: 'I'm so cold.'

The moment Nikki was evicted from the *Big Brother* house, she made front-page headlines in the *News of the World* with saucy pics of her previous incarnation as an escort girl. Not surprisingly, it didn't damage her chance of cashing in, and the clock is already ticking on her guaranteed 15 minutes of fame. While Nikki and Pete are paraded as the new Chantelle and Preston, the jury is out on how long the relationship can last. As Pete gets set to launch a pop career, Nikki has already completed her first TV series for E4 called *Princess Nikki*. Anyone who watches it deserves to have their privates removed and boiled in oil before their very eyes.

10
Is It Just Me or Are Boys Better At It?

Reality TV's winners and losers

Jade, Chantelle and Nikki are famous and have already amassed a fortune from their stints on reality TV. But it's the boys who take the lead when it comes to lasting the test of time by carving a niche for themselves as celebrities after their initial reality TV exposure.

WILL YOUNG

We have to make the distinction between making it as a pop star and the earning potential that goes with it – and working consistently in television and the media. If we judge it on earnings alone, then Will Young wins hands down. But let's not forget that Will wanted to win *Pop Idol* so badly; he had the talent, yes, but moreover Will had the will to win. He was desperate for fame. He knew how to handle the press, he came out at the right time and has never (as yet) been the subject of any scandal. He is the perfect winner.

Making it as a pop star is never just about being able to sing well – it's about stage presence, image, performance and taking the right advice about the material you choose. In this case, Will made many of the right choices right from the start – he decided not to sign with Simon Cowell and do an album of covers; instead, he recorded his own songs and had some good ones written for him.

BEN FOGLE

 Ben first found fame by participating in the BBC reality show *Castaway* in 2000. Since then, the blue-eyed toff has presented *One Man and His Dog*, *Animal Park* and *Countryfile*, and seems ever willing to appear in our living rooms wearing less and less clothing. Most notably, he rowed across the Atlantic in the company of Olympic oarsman James Cracknell and made a TV documentary about the ordeal, which, for much of the time, he and his strapping partner undertook naked. Their claim was that the sea water would cause nasty chafing if they were to wear

anything. We're not stupid, Ben! How else could you guarantee millions of female (and male) viewers for a TV show – *Through Hell and High Water* – about rowing across an ocean for seven weeks? The only suspense involved was whether we'd get a glimpse of an Olympic buttock, or a loose pair of Fogle's knackers.

Given the publicity the pair received – the rowers, not the buttocks – this strategy worked like a charm. After coming third in the race, all buttocks and knackers were found to be in full working order. And the spin-off publicity has been masterfully handled, with TV programmes and book launches stacked up for weeks afterwards.

With his boyish good looks, the enthusiasm of a Golden Retriever puppy, his posh voice and his ever-so-slight speech impediment, Ben is made for TV. He also makes a good living as a travel writer. Ben is one those likeable guys who is a natural on TV, and he has an army of female and gay fans. With that sort of support, his further 'exposure' on TV is guaranteed.

FRAN COSGRAVE

Fran actually became famous for appearing on reality TV shows. Prior to that he owned nightclubs and found his way into the tabloids for having had a number of famous girlfriends, including model Jodie Marsh and Atomic Kitten singer Natasha Hamilton, with whom he has one son, Josh. He is a former security guard of the boyband Westlife.

In 2004, Cosgrave was a contestant on the ITV reality TV show *I'm a Celebrity, Get Me Out of Here!* finishing third. Due to appearing on this show, he managed to raise £117,000 for Temple Street Children's Hospital in Dublin. Prior to this, he had a small amount of exposure thanks to his girlfriends, but many viewers would not have considered him a celebrity even if they had heard of him. In 2005, he appeared in another ITV reality show, *Celebrity Love Island*, which he went on to win alongside Jayne Middlemiss.

BRIAN DOWLING

Brian may not be constantly in the headlines since he won *Big Brother 2* in 2001. What he has done is secure the right management to ensure he has worked consistently as a TV presenter ever since. When Brian first appeared on *BB*, he was working as an air steward for Ryanair. He was quickly signed up by Blaze Television and presented *SM:TV* for which he won two BAFTA awards. Brian is both charismatic and stylish and says, 'I'm proudest of my ability to talk to anyone, anywhere. It's what I'm famous for.'

He is also consistently voted the most popular *Big Brother* contestant, and he has that innate ability to be lovably camp, without shoving it down your throat. Now there's a blessing.

PAUL DANAN

Love Island's Paul Danan wasn't everyone's cup of tea and was seen as a bit of a lecherous ladies man – but that hasn't done him any harm. It's fair to point out that Paul had previously been in *Hollyoaks,* so this made him a minor celeb. As celebrities go, he's not exactly in the Beckham stakes, but you have to start somewhere. Press interest escalated after he shared a bed with the American model Nikki Ziering, sparking speculation that the couple had sex on the resort.

He is one of the UK's biggest 'minor' celebrities and continues to stay on the periphery of the public's mind. He just needs that one juicy scandal – a sex change, perhaps, or a high-profile arrest while dogging – to really shoot him up the celebrity rankings.

JEFF BRAZIER

Jeff is worth mentioning again simply because he is one of those people who works within his scope. He doesn't take on anything too ambitious and he never stops working. Since appearing on C4's *Shipwrecked* and then winning *The Farm* in 2004, he has worked steadily on the fringes of real popularity and recognition. His love links to Jade will ensure he is never out of the spotlight, and he will always have the public's sympathy for having known Jade – intimately – before her outing as a megastar.

11
How to Get on Reality TV

It's never been easier to get on TV.
Here is just a snapshot of some of the current and future reality
TV programme ideas that require desperate wannabes:

Looking to Buy a Home?
We want first-time buyers who have no clue about how to get on the first rung of the ladder. The stupider the better.

Want to Mend Your Marriage?
With our nationally accredited experts, we will probe into the deepest recesses of your marriage, pull it to bits, and then expose your deepest, darkest secrets on national television.

Want to Build a Custom Car?
Why bother keeping your old banger going when you could spend a couple of days hammering away at the

bodywork of a 1982 Ford Orion, and turn it into a 1982 Ford Orion with bits of chrome stuck all over it.

Had a Wild Wedding?

Did you and your partner do something that you'll regret for the rest of your lives? Want to share it with us? Did you get married naked, or make all your guests fly out to Hawaii, and then you all got holed up in a basement for three days because of a tropical storm? We want to hear from you, if you're capable of using a phone, of course.

Looking to Rebuild Your Relationship?

We'll help you rebuild the tattered remains of your relationship, and if we can't, we'll at least capture you screaming and throwing things at each other, so you will always have that as a reminder of your love after you're divorced.

Want to Change Your Child's Diet?

Does your little angel live off deep-fried Mars bars and 2-litre bottles of Coca-Cola? You need our expert nutritionist, who will make you look really stupid and accuse you of child abuse, and will then force your child to eat puréed spinach for three months. Watch how their behaviour changes…and how no one else in your neighbourhood will talk to you.

Want to Makeover Your Spouse?

Is your partner a real minger? Why not call in our crack team of DIY experts, who used to work on a home makeover show, but that went out of fashion, so now they plaster, skim and reroof people instead.

Have You Got a Possession with a Hidden History?

Are you too lazy to get down to the Antiques Roadshow? Do you want us to come round to you and value your junk-shop tat instead? If you have something that you think is worth a bit, then whatever you do, don't advertise the fact on national telly. You'll be burgled within a week, and you probably won't have got off your arse to get it insured properly.

Have You Got Britain's Next Best Recipe?

Do you see yourself as a modern-day Fanny, or a chilled-out Gordon Ramsay? Have you got a recipe for sardine and mandarin fritters that your friends say they love? Whatever you bung in a pot, we'll film it and then get a TV chef to spit it out in disgust in front of millions. Go on, get cooking!

What are you waiting for? There are as many different types of reality shows as there are people watching them, so you have no excuse for not getting yourself on telly. But before you pick up the phone, you first need to know exactly how should you present yourself when auditioning for a reality TV show.

Beonscreen.com is just one of many talent-search websites that, in just two years on the Internet, has become to TV research teams what eBay is to ticket touts. The makers of *Wife Swap*, *Families at War* and *Big Brother* have all posted vacancies on the site. So if there's one site that you must look at, it's this one.

But before you sign up, you will want to impress the producers of the TV shows and listen to what the experts have to say. Here is the top advice from reality TV casting directors. Remember, they are looking for people who can hold an hour of TV, so there has to be something special about you that people want to watch.

They are *not* looking for actors. In fact, any TV experience or appearing on a previous reality TV show almost certainly will get you cut from the short list. They're looking for fresh faces, new, genuine people – 'real' life – not aspiring actors.

It doesn't matter how old, how beautiful, how tall, how skinny you are – none of that matters. You have to be different, quirky, funny and have plenty of energy.

Programmes like *Big Brother* run 24/7, so if you're always in bed early, you'll be left behind – the cameras will be on those who are awake.

Most casting directors will ask you a ton of questions, and they are looking for people who can speak well. (Although in Jade and Chantelle's case, the casting directors just needed to know that they could speak.) Your accent doesn't matter but you have to be able to make yourself understood. Don't mutter. Speak up. Have energy. Make them laugh. A typical casting director or producer will give you about two minutes of their time. If you can't entertain for two minutes on screen, how will you entertain an audience for an hour?

Before you even get to that point of talking to producers or casting agents, you have to spend a little time on your application. Make sure you have a good photo that can be shown to network executives – not a fuzzy snapshot of you cuddling up to a stripper at a stag do. On the other hand, don't send a formal head shot either because it's a dead cert that you're just another aspiring actor looking for a break. A shot from waist up with you looking directly at the camera is a good choice. Unless the back of your head is your best side. If that's the case, then don't bother applying anyway. Dress as if you're going to job interview or church.

If you send in a video tape, don't be afraid to be yourself. You don't have to be gorgeous but show your smile, personality and sparkle. Most reality TV shows put contestants in situations that bring out the best or worst in people. Some producers are looking for people who will make good before and after pictures, for instance. The US reality show *Queer Eye for the Straight Guy* obviously won't choose people who look like they've got their act together from day one – they need to see the potential for some improvement, but they also won't consider you if you look like you're from the Addams family. The programme has to be an hour long, and they'll want to end on some kind of successful transformation, so they won't want to bite off more than they can chew.

In elimination shows like *The Apprentice*, the casting directors are looking for the types of people who are bound to create drama, and drama comes about through conflict, when two or more people want different things. In most cases, plenty of the drama is set up in the rules of the reality show, i.e., one person is voted off each week as in *Survivor* or *Big Brother*. On top of that, though, the show needs to be interesting and watchable outside the competition element, so they are looking for people who will naturally conflict when you put them in the same room or house together.

But, like everything, there's a balance to be struck. Producers don't want too much drama. Drug references, alcohol, criminal records, ex-convicts – these are elements that casting directors naturally avoid. And before anyone gets on TV, there will be ample background checks, so don't bother lying. Make sure you are what they're looking for or choose another show to audition for.

The most attractive applicants to reality-show makers are people who are accessible emotionally but also stable, people who are open and willing to share. They avoid people who are lazy and might not show up for interviews. That rings warning bells immediately, as those people might not bother to put their all into the show on screen, or might be inclined to drop out when the going gets a bit tougher.

Remember, even though producers know you have a life and a job, they're used to working with actors who bend over backwards for them and who are prepared to be shafted by anyone and everyone, while smiling and saying, 'Thanks, it was a pleasure working with you.' So that's what they're expecting from you – attentiveness and commitment. You have to be on the ball, ready for anything, flexible, and easy to get on with. 'Cos if you're not, there are thousands out there who are.

Most shows have a lengthy interview process. You'll have appointments to keep, ample forms to fill out and papers to sign. Make sure you do all that promptly, even if you have to rush an application form or type a quick reply to the producer's sudden emails.

A Channel 4 executive said, 'I've waited and waited for applications, photos or biogs from people who I thought were perfect candidates, but we ended up choosing others because they didn't reply right away. Promptness wins. I would take a poorly or quickly filled out response to one that's taking for ever any day of the week.'

If you are selected for a reality TV show, remember that there is a great deal of money being invested at that point. So casting directors are watching for signs of flaky attitudes or 'flight risks' – people who change their minds about wanting to be on the show or who will suddenly decide to do something else. So you have to be prepared to stick with it for the long haul, present yourself with a certain amount of maturity, and really enjoy the process of being part of a reality TV show. If you're just doing it for the fame or the money, then you'll probably fail.

TOP TIPS FOR REALITY TV STARDOM

DO ask yourself whether you're really cut out for reality TV

DO think carefully about the type of show that will show you off best

DO your homework – watch the shows, or research what has worked on the Internet

DO get advice and critical feedback from friends and family

DO show off your personality

DO have energy

DO speak clearly

DO spend time on the application and do exactly what it asks

DO be prompt and follow up

DO be different – but not too different; gimmicky or tacky won't work

DO be prepared to do whatever the producers want (within legal limits)

DON'T always trust what they say – be realistic

DON'T send photos of you in your underwear

DON'T tell them about your acting experience or aspirations – lie

DON'T ask for your fee up front; you'll be ejected by security

12
The Freak Factor

If you've got it, flaunt it

While the A-list earners walk off into reality sunset to land the next dream job, let's spare a thought for the freaks. They're the ones who help viewing figures sag to new lows as they masturbate pigs, urinate live in the jungle or flash their privates in the *Big Brother* house. There are two compelling aspects to reality TV – the winners and the losers. Those we love and those we love to hate.

When the line-up was announced for *Celebrity Big Brother* in 2005, the tabloids targeted Michael Barrymore as the one to loathe. But once the programme was aired, the focus of freakery fell on Jodie

Marsh, Pete Burns and George Galloway, with Barrymore redeeming himself in the eyes of the viewers to become runner-up to Chantelle.

So what ingredients make up the freakiest of freaky in celebrity land? Is it the fact that Pete Burns looks like he's been hit in the face several times with a saucepan, and been caught in an explosion in the Mary Quant factory? Or is it that he wears split-crotch knickers and rubber halter-necks? Or is it that he's one of the bitchiest, foul-mouthed, vicious housemates ever to appear on *Big Brother*? Pete Burns says, 'I saw plastic surgery totally as a way of using flesh as fabric to create something...' That may well be, Pete, but we can virtually see that fabric bursting at the seams, and it's no coincidence that when you cross your legs, your mouth snaps open. You freak!

Or is the freakery down to what celebs are prepared to do on telly to remain in the public eye...or what they think they can get away with, despite being surrounded by more cameras than at a Premiership football match? Carol Thatcher may have thought she was safe dropping her knickers and weeing in the dead of night in the jungle, but she forgot the joy of infra-red night vision. Or did she? Perhaps it was just a brilliant masterstroke from someone whom the public had thought was a reality TV innocent. Having a jimmy on telly was perhaps not terribly attractive viewing – anyone drinking apple juice at the time would probably have gagged – but she won the show, and her unashamed loo break must have had something to do with it. Her mother must have been so proud!

On the first *Celebrity Big Brother*, Vanessa Feltz was peculiarly affected by her surroundings, and the nuttiness of Chris Eubank. Eventually, she was reduced to scrawling crazed ramblings on the dining table, and was the second housemate to be evicted. The public loves freakish behaviour, but not when it's from a blobby chat-show host.

And talking of unstable, pneumatic breasts of all shapes and sizes are firmly established in the 'freak-show' category. The great British public is permanently obsessed with body contouring, expanding, sucking, tweaking, enlarging, reducing, smoothing and plucking, and there's no end of celebs on offer to satisfy their lust. Lea Walker from *Big Brother 7* claims to have the largest breast implants in the UK – she went from 30AA to 30M over four boob jobs. What's more worrying is that she

thinks it's attractive, when she obviously looks like an victim of fall-out at Chernobyl.

Someone else who deserves to be welcomed into the Academy of Freaks – and could perhaps be elected as High Priestess – is Jackie Stallone, who appeared briefly on *Celebrity Big Brother*. It's difficult to know where to start when you examine the evidence of freakery – the lips…the drawl…the sheer ugliness of a face that looks like its been sat on by a hippo…the 'paranormal' abilities she claims to have…the fact that she's Sylvester Stallone's mum, and mother-in-law to Brigitte Nielsen…she's rich, and she treats people like dirt…let's face it, Jackie's got it all. So if you're thinking of becoming a bit of a freak yourself, then you've got a long way to go to top this particular walking circus act.

GETTING IT WRONG

Having the freak factor is all well and good but you need a little more to sustain you if you are to be imprisoned in the *Big Brother* house for three months. It's very easy to get it wrong. Kinga masturbating with a bottle didn't exactly win her votes, though that is what she will be remembered for.

Obviously, in the case of a *Celebrity Big Brother*, those who once had a profile – Pete Burns and Barrymore, for example – have the chance to redeem themselves and win back their own fan base at the same time as attracting a new audience, though for Barrymore and Pete Burns it didn't happen. Pete ended up in rehab and Barrymore in New Zealand.

You, as an unknown TV wannabe, need to start from scratch to win the public votes and stay on telly. You will have to have your wits about you and have a strategy that ensures you last the game. Chantelle is a fine example of how an unknown wannabe celeb can win over established has-beens. She gave the audience what they wanted. She was also a natural, and a fame virgin.

People like Pete Doherty, Rik Waller, John Leslie and Nadia Almada (the transgender winner of *Big Brother 5*) are obvious examples of how to get it wrong. They abused the fame game by not adhering to the rules. Rik Waller had his moment by singing to 10 million people. Why did he then start bad-mouthing Simon Cowell? John Leslie had a great job on TV, loads of fans, a big house and a fat salary. His sex drive took over and he lost his focus and his job. Sex and drugs attracts headlines – big ones – but they don't always further a career.

Nadia got infected with the 'Don't you know who I am?' virus, for which there is no known cure. She then fell foul of the law.

Pete Doherty may be a hero to some but given the amount of tabloid headlines he has garnered he should be a millionaire by now. He's not – he's in debt.

If you're lucky enough to achieve celebrity status, the hard work has only just begun. Your public persona needs constant tending and nurturing...otherwise it could all go horribly wrong. You must never forget yourself for a minute. The mistake many celebrities make is that once they ascend to the dizzy heights of fame and wealth, they believe that they are untouchable. Why do you think Max Clifford's phone never stops ringing? Celebrity is big business and there's big money to be made if you get it right.

We can learn how to do it from those who get it

right, but equally how not to do it from those who make huge PR blunders and literal cock-ups.

LESLIE GRANTHAM

Admittedly, he's not likely to work at the RSC or will ever win an Oscar, but for many years he was the nation's favourite baddie. His pulling power in terms of ratings for *EastEnders* has never been equalled; so the bosses at the Beeb wheeled him back in. Grantham must have felt as though he owned Albert Square. In fact, he was so comfortable in his reign as the returning King of Walford that he indulged in a little five-fingered shuffle in his dressing room in 2004 via a webcam.

The images of Leslie Grantham enjoying himself in front of his computer is imprinted on the minds of the nation. He was suspended from work but was eventually allowed back after he apologised.

In 2005, 16.2 million viewers tuned in to watch Dirty Den's final demise at the hands of his wife Chrissie with a doorstop. Grantham's departure was reported to be because of the adverse publicity generated by the 'unsavoury activities' in his dressing room, although the actor stated that he left because he didn't want his contract renewed.

RICHARD BACON

In 1997, *Blue Peter* installed a new, fresh-faced, cocky lad to get down with the kids and make more things out of toilet rolls twice a week on the BBC.

He goes down in *Blue Peter* history for being the only presenter in the programme's lengthy history to have his contract terminated. After just 18 months, a Sunday tabloid exposed his penchant for cocaine – not the ideal image for a children's presenter. The then head of BBC children's programmes went on air to explain the situation to the kids!

Remarkably, Bacon is still in huge demand as a TV and radio presenter, almost because of the scandal. He has presented *This Morning*, *Top of the Pops*, *Back to Reality* and had radio shows on Capital, XFM and BBC Five Live.

MICHAEL BARRYMORE

Troubled comedian Michael Barrymore was the king (and queen) of Saturday night TV. Barrymore's life can be read through a trail of tacky tabloid tales. His TV shows were watched by 20 million viewers but he became a victim of his own success. Drink and drugs were never too far away and, on 31 March 2001, meat-factory worker Stuart Lubbock died after being found floating motionless in Barrymore's swimming pool during a party at his house. His body had high levels of narcotics and alcohol as well as anal injuries. Many tabloid newspapers accused Barrymore of holding drug-fuelled gay orgies in his home and asserted that he must have had some responsibility for the lad's death, though he was never charged with an offence.

PAULA ABDUL

In 2005, the former pop star and choreographer, while serving as a judge on talent show *American Idol*, was alleged to have had a sexual encounter with contestant and wannabe Corey Clark. The FOX Network announced that it had carried out a thorough investigation and had cleared Abdul of all charges levied by Clark.

WOODY ALLEN

In 1992, the film director split from his long-term partner Mia Farrow after she discovered that he'd been having an affair. And not just with some mystery busty blonde. He'd been allegedly at it with her adopted daughter Soon-Yi Previn, who was 35 years younger than Allen. There was a media outcry and the tabloids hounded the odd couple.

HEATHER MILLS-MCCARTNEY

She's the peace activist and 'porn' model – although her publicist insists she was snapped simulating sex for a 'lover's guide' – who survived a horrific accident and captured the heart of a Beatle. A word of warning, though, if you're willing to chase down fame at all costs – make sure you have a skeleton-free closet, or at least secure that closet with some really strong padlocks. Heather had everything a girl could want until those pics appeared in the *News of the World*. According to Max Clifford, 'Everyone knew Heather had a past...'

FRANK BOUGH

The dear, lovable TV presenter who has gently guided us through the 1970s–80s telling us all about consumer pitfalls and reporting on sport, had his TV career endangered by a colourful private life, including allegations of wearing lingerie at sex parties while using cocaine. As our world turned upside-down, there were many who thought, 'Frank, you cheeky minx...good on ya!' His career, though, was doomed.

GEORGE MICHAEL

In 1998, the singer was arrested for engaging in a lewd act in a public toilet in Beverly Hills. Despite an initial outcry, Michael went on TV and explained it away, and even joked about it in his single 'Outside'. He got away relatively unscathed in terms of his public image, and he did a great deal for the profile of public toilets in the States.

But then in 2006 there were pictures of him slumped at the wheel of his 4 x 4 in the middle of the road in the early hours. What had been going on? It was claimed that he had been smoking cannabis. A helpful passer-by managed to take a few pictures, and it was a case of 'wake me up before you go go' to the press.

When it happened again, people began to think that George was on a self-destruct mission. And later in 2006, it was reported that he had had a rummage around in the bushes of a London park with another gentleman. Yet the British public don't seem to be too shocked by these revelations any more. It's now almost accepted that some celebs have dinner at The Ivy, some get drunk in gentlemen's clubs and throw up outside, and George likes to go to Hampstead Heath for a bit of a roll around in the bushes. Things ain't what they used to be.

13
From Popstars *to* The X Factor

*'I've nothing against anyone following
their dreams – but not if they're crap.'*
ROBBIE WILLIAMS

While George Michael finds solace in the bushes, there are thousands of wannabe pop stars queueing up to audition for *The X Factor* and to be verbally assaulted by Simon Cowell. While Will Young goes from strength to strength, he leaves behind a tacky trail of pop hopefuls who have taken Simon's advice to hang on to their day job.

Singing talent contests lead the ratings war in reality TV land. *American Idol*'s audience has grown to around 35 million viewers every week in the US, while *The X Factor* gets 10 million viewers in Britain.

In the beginning, there was *Popstars*. But one click on the One True Voice website tells you everything that happened – nothing. If you dream of being the next

165

Will Young or Kelly Clarkson, then make sure that a) you can sing and b) you have thick skin. Pop is a rocky road. Hear'Say had their ten minutes of fame with only two survivors – Kym Marsh and Myleene Klass – still out there making a living. There is an exception to every rule, though, and the Cheeky Girls are living proof that there are no rules when it comes to making it big. They may have no credibility as performers, talent or sex appeal, but they're still on our screens and earning a living. There's no justice, is there?

If you don't listen to the right, advice winning a reality music show can be a one way ticket to Nowhereville…economy class. But those Girls Aloud minxes have gone from strength to strength since trouncing the boys on *Popstars: The Rivals*. A killer first album saw them go straight from check out girls to chart-toppers and they haven't looked back since. Now they're dripping in celeb boyfriends and tabloid chit-chat about scraps with toilet attendants, and it's fair to say they've officially made it mostly thanks to sound management, good songs and good looks. They remain the only successful band to have come out of a reality TV show.

On 5 October 2001, it was goodbye to Nasty Nigel and hello to Simon Cowell. ITV launched *Pop Idol* and the rest is history – along with Gareth Gates and Michelle McManus. *Pop Idol* was a great TV format and produced a number of fun acts including Darius

Danesh, who enjoyed minor chart success and is now moving and shaking in the world of musical theatre, having starred in *Chicago* as Billy Flynn in 2006.

In 2002 in the US, the FOX television network was seduced by the success of *Pop Idol* and signed up Simon Cowell to front *American Idol* which turned out to be quite a cute decision. With over 30,000 pop hopefuls turning up to the first auditions in Chicago, *American Idol* was soon attracting 30 million viewers every week. It is now America's highest rated show with the *Idol* brand going global.

Then the BBC came up with *Fame Academy*. Although it was viewed by critics as being very similar to the *Pop Idol* and *Popstars* series, and was generally classified as an entertainment programme, it was presented as a relatively new concept. It went head-to-head with *Pop Idol* and lost. The show produced two flagship series, and the eventual winners were David Sneddon and Alex Parks, both of whom have produced relatively successful albums, but who have struggled to match the staying power and celebrity clout of Lemar Obika, the sensational soul singer from London. He came third in the first series, has since stormed to the top of the charts, and has so far won two Brits, two MOBOs and sold 1.5 million albums. Not bad for a bronze medallist!

The X Factor is the ultimate reality TV talent contest. It has all the ingredients – people who can't sing but think they can, people who can sing and think they can't, and judges who are more competitive and bitchy than the competitors. Today, if you want to get an audition on *The X Factor*, you'll have to put in quite a bit of effort. In recent series, over 100,000 applied. In 2005, winner Shayne Ward, a former shoe-shop assistant, Andy Abraham, a former bin man and the duo Journey South went on to have platinum-selling albums. The jury is out as to whether they'll last another year.

To compete against Simon Cowell and *The X Factor*, the BBC will need to do better than *How Do You Solve a Problem Like Maria*? It just doesn't have the same broad appeal – and it's a problem few really cared about, particularly when it was so obvious that the main purpose of the show was to line the pockets of the producers of the West End show, and a certain Mr A Lloyd-Webber.

TOP TEN CELEBRITY HELLRAISERS

KEITH RICHARDS

'There's a demon in me, and he's still around. Without the dope, we have a bit more of a chat these days.'

COURTNEY LOVE

'You know, I am cool. I just am.'

OZZY OSBOURNE

'I'm the Prince of fucking Darkness...It's good fun and it's had great rewards. It's been such an eye opener for me. Everything that I have ever wanted to have has come from rock 'n' roll. I've had happiness, I've had sadness. I've had everything. I've experienced life, death, birth, marriage, divorce, and it's been a whole bunch of fun. I wouldn't have it any different. I'd do it all again tomorrow.'

PETE DOHERTY

'One minute I'm waiting for Kate to arrive to join me in the jacuzzi for a romantic evening. The next thing I can remember is doing cold turkey in a vomit-filled cell.'

SHAUN RYDER

'I'm here to harass you, I want your pills and your grass you, You don't look first class you, Let me look up your ass you...'

TOMMY LEE

'I also did some jail time a few years ago. Spent a whole summer in jail reading books. I pumped a ton of new knowledge and new thinking into myself.'

JOHNNY ROTTEN

'I'm no one's lap dog, you can't put me on a leash.'

ROBBIE WILLIAMS

'I'm a bit of a slag...Some people don't think it's very nice, but I don't care... I've got hormones, and sex is there, so why not? Sex is good. Everybody does it, and everybody should!'

CHARLOTTE CHURCH

'I am at that age when former child stars go off the rails.'

LIAM GALLAGHER

'I need them, need them to give me a kick up the arse. Otherwise I'd just be sat in getting fat, counting me money. It's good people living on your doorstep and looking through your bins. Gives you energy.'

14
Where Are They Now?

It's a little dangerous to assume that an appearance on *The X Factor* will automatically secure you a lifetime of fame, fortune and dedicated groupies. For many, it can be ten seconds of reality fame, six months of nightclub personal appearances and a subsequent eternity of not even being recognised by your own mother. But if you *really* can sing, then go for it, but only if you are determined to succeed at all costs.

Looking at our chart of survivors from the music reality shows, maybe it's not all about winning the show that counts. The real winners are the losers – if you want to aim for a long-term career in showbiz, then make sure you're a runner-up.

DAVID SNEDDON

Deserved winner of the first series of *Fame Academy* in 2004. Had a Number One single with 'Stop Living the Lie' and a top five album. He's now a song writer signed to Universal. This guy has talent but lacks charisma, and could do with a *News of the World* journo going through his bins and finding some sleaze – in his case, it would probably be something along the lines of getting a parking ticket, or enjoying the odd Twix.

Earnings rating: ★★★

ALEX PARKS

Winner of the second series of *Fame Academy*. She reached Number Three with her first single, the self-penned 'Maybe That's What It Takes'. She also had a massive amount of street cred and tabloid attention for admitting that she came from Cornwall...and that she was gay. Her début album *Introduction* was subsequently released and sold over 500,000 copies. Following a row over distribution with her record label Polydor, Alex is 'resting'. The future now looks bleak.

Earnings rating: ★★

STEVE BROOKSTEIN

Winner of the first series of *The X Factor*. His cover of *Against All Odds* reached Number One in the UK chart, although it only stayed there for one week. He donated all proceeds to the Thailand Tsunami Disaster Fund. His first album *Heart & Soul* made its debut at the top of the UK album chart in May 2005 and sold 150,000 copies.

Steve hasn't been lucky. The press don't like him and he no longer has a recording contract with Sony BMG. He has been working on a second album, on which one of the tracks is called 'Can't Get Any Worse Than This...'

Earnings rating: ★★

CHICO

A semi-finalist on second series of *The X Factor*, Chico was mentored enthusiastically by Sharon Osbourne. He released his début single 'It's Chico Time' in February 2006, and it remained at Number One for two weeks. Chico's follow-up single, a cover of the song 'DISCO' entered the charts at Number Twenty-Four the following August. Chico's cheekiness and six-pack are popular with the girls, but don't expect too may more number-one hits. Beats being a goat herder, though.

Earnings rating: ★★

THE CHEEKY GIRLS

Monica and Gabriela Irimia shot to fame after appearing on *Popstars: the Rivals*. Nobody thought they had a cat in hell's chance. Luckily, they had a mum who was a tad more than cheeky. In January 2004, their first single, 'The Cheeky Song (Touch my Bum)', written by their mum, was voted the worst pop record of all time in a Channel 4 poll, despite spending five weeks in the top five in the UK singles chart, and peaking at Number Two for four (non-consecutive) weeks. Losers win again.

Sadly, On 4 August 2006, London newspaper the *Evening Standard* reported that the Cheeky Girls were 'at rock bottom' and were facing bankruptcy action in court due the fact they had not been paid by their now defunct record company Telstar Records. The article said that the girls owed £4,500 in unpaid taxes, along with other bills due, and that Telstar owed them £2.2 million.

Earnings rating: ★

DARIUS DANESH

A brilliant example of tenacity and self-belief...or outrageous arrogance? After *Pop Idol*, he refused to sign for Simon Cowell's record label, preferring the management skills of Simon Fuller. His first self-penned single, 'Colourblind', entered the UK singles chart at Number One, and his début album went platinum. A best-selling autobiography followed and he has broken into the mainstream musical theatre industry as well.

Darius knows how to get the best out of the media and remains a strong supporter of The Prince's Trust.

He has celebrated five Top Ten charting UK singles. He is still managed by Simon Fuller, and has enjoyed a great career so far for a 'loser' of a reality TV show. Earnings rating: ★★★★

MICHELLE MCMANUS

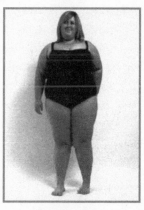

Michelle won the second series of *Pop Idol* despite the judges' initial opinion that she was too overweight to be a pop star. Pete Waterman was so disappointed with Michelle's victory that he left the studio in the subsequent advertisement break after the announcement was made. The first single 'All This Time' arrived at Number One on the UK singles chart in January 2004 and stayed there for three weeks. Predictably, once the hype had died down, Michelle's star has waned considerably, and she's most recently been seen on *You Are What You Eat*, and suffering the indignity of having Gillian McKeith poking about in her poo. She did lose 5 stone, though, and could end up being telly's biggest celebrity loser. Earnings rating: ★★

GARETH GATES

Gareth won the nation's hearts on *Pop Idol*, only coming second to Will Young by a couple of votes. But it has been Will who has shown impressive staying power, and who has used his talent and public profile very cleverly to maintain his A-list status. And all that despite Simon Cowell's view that Gareth would be a more enduring pop idol.

Gareth isn't exactly on skid row, though – he's had Number One singles in twelve countries, so don't feel too sorry for him. He has earned good money and remains a great example of the power of reality TV, and he's reputedly had a romp with Jordan. Maybe that's why he looks like he's had all the life sucked out of him. A documentary about his roller coaster flirt with fame is also on the cards.

Earnings rating: ★★★★

LIBERTY X

Richard Branson signed them up, and things looked good for them with three Top Five albums. Now they're definitely on the way out, unless something truly miraculous occurs, but they have had a career from reality TV and made money.

Earnings rating: ★★★★

RIK WALLER

Told by Simon Cowell on the first series of *Pop Idol* that he was 'too much of a twat to be an idol' and his pulling out of the competition led to Darius Dinesh being allowed into the final. Following the show, Rik signed a one-album contract with EMI worth

£400,000, with his first single being a cover of Dolly Parton's *I Will Always Love You*.

He has since taken part in *Celebrity Fit Club* and *Back to Reality*. On *Celebrity Fit Club*, it emerged that Rik had a body fat content of around 60 per cent, which is hardly surprising given the fact he eats around 35 meals a day. His career, unlike his weight, is in freefall.
Earnings rating: ★★

HEAR'SAY

Hear'Say's first single, *Pure and Simple*, went straight to Number One in the UK singles chart in March 2001. Hear'Say officially split up on 1 October 2002, citing negative public reaction as the main reason. Who said the British public always gets it wrong? Kym Marsh, Myleene Klass and Suzanne Shaw, however, continue to attract headlines and work.
Earnings rating: ★★★

ONE TRUE VOICE

Their début single 'Sacred Trust/After You're Gone' went head-to-head with Girls Aloud on 16 December 2002 for the Christmas Number One spot. One True Voice lost out to the girls and had to settle for the Number Two position. Since then, Matt auditioned unsuccessfully for *The X Factor* in 2004 and Keith has re-formed his pre-OTV band, the Keith Semple Band. Jamie has dabbled in a bit of TV presenting on local Welsh television. As far as the band is concerned,

though, the Voice is in need of some really strong cough drops if we're ever going to hear from it again.
Earnings rating: ★

LEMAR

Came third in the first series of *Fame Academy* and has never looked back. Went on to sign for Sony Records and is still enjoying chart success. First single 'Dance with U' reached Number 2 on the UK singles charts in 2003. His first album, *Dedicated*, was released late in 2003. As we've learnt already, Lemar has a great deal of credibility in the music industry and is a long way from being a one-hit wonder. As a main headliner at various festivals and gigs, and with his own tour as well, he can only go from strength to strength.
Earnings rating: ★★★★

BRENDA EDWARDS

The last female standing in the second series of *The X Factor* has been living the dream in London's West End as the star of the hit show *Chicago*. With good management, Brenda will now work consistently. She may not be Number One in the pop charts, but she's doing what she's always wanted to do, and she's got a belting voice that should earn her a solid career.
Earnings rating: ★★★

MARIA LAWSON

Maria, who was controversially voted off the second

series of *The X Factor* could easily have slipped under everyone's radar, never to be heard of again. But on 6 March 2006, Maria announced that she had signed to the Sony BMG record label. Her début single 'Sleepwalking' was released on 14 August and has been well received, entering the UK chart at Number 20. Earnings rating: ★★

TEENAGE CELEBRITY RICH LIST

DANIEL RADCLIFFE – £23M

The speccy hero from *Harry Potter* has led an enchanted life since landing the role as the wimpy wizard. Now seen in cameo roles on such hit shows as Ricky Gervais's *Extras*, he's got a long and lucrative career beckoning.

JOSS STONE – £9M

She sings like an angel, looks like a supermodel, writes her own material and has won Brits, Grammys…and she's still only 19! Guaranteed mega-stardom, and she thoroughly deserves it.

LILY COLE – £8M

Blue eyes, red hair, 'elfin' features, she looks like a china doll, *and* aced her Cambridge University interview…she was never going to flip burgers in McDonald's for a living, was she?

RUPERT GRINT – £5M

He's a freckly, red-haired sidekick (he plays Ron Weasley, Harry Potter's best friend), but the *Harry Potter* films have made him a big name in his own right. The awkward lummox has made some smart career moves in recent times, and is sure to become part of the UK acting élite at some point.

EMMA WATSON – £5M

Nobody likes a know-it-all? Not so in Emma's case. Having emerged as a genuinely engaging actress in the *Harry Potter* series, Emma has also grown from ugly-duckling beginnings to her new image as a very attractive and sophisticated swan. The future's bright for the girl with the swollen bank account.

JAMIE BELL – £2M

Since his eye-catching performance in the film of *Billy Elliot*, Jamie has had the world at his feet, culminating most recently in a film for Clint Eastwood. Now in his twenties, his days of prancing around in tights are probably numbered.

MCFLY – £1M EACH

They can sing, play instruments and they're rich! They're Britain's hottest boyband at the moment, and it looks like they'll be sticking around for a while yet. McFlying high!

15
The Ups and Downs of Being Famous

'I didn't really want to be famous.'
PARIS HILTON

THE IMPORTANCE OF BEING IN REHAB

Being famous has both its upside and its downside. Every day, the cash registers at The Priory 'ker-chingggg' as another pop star or actor checks out after treatment. It's not just drink and drugs, either. Treatment for anger management, depression and suicidal tendencies all figure on the á la carte rehab menu.

The latest must-have package is called 'Equine Assisted Psychotherapy', in which a horse called Guinness 'helps people with drug and alcohol problems to overcome their addictions. Equine Assisted Psychotherapy (EAP) is being used for the first time in a clinical setting in England by the Priory Hospital North London.' The medical director at the hospital has stated that horses are a 'wonderful tool' in helping patients get through to their emotions very quickly. Presumably, for patients suffering from a gambling addiction, there's always the bonus of having a quick flutter on whether the horse will help to cure anyone.

Rehab is big business and a must do for celebs on the way up or down. You've not really made it until you've suffered a bit of personal torment for which you've had to have a bit of therapy.

So what are the pressures of being famous? Most of us believe that being a star is all about the glamour and the beautiful life, about having everything that your heart could desire. There's nothing that a celeb would want and couldn't possibly get. Their position as million-grossing public figures grants them access to a world of which most of us can only dream. But does all this come at too high a price?

For most celebs, rehab clinics have become like a second home, a place where they inevitably end up at one point or another in their career. Michael Barrymore is top of our celebrity rehab list – he's been admitted nine times. Maybe he needs rehab to treat his addiction to rehab. So what makes today's celebs like Pete Doherty abuse drugs and alcohol to such an extent?

Pete Doherty has made headlines in all the tabloids. In March 2006, not a day went by without him being mentioned for some kind of drug arrest, car theft or alcohol-fuelled night out. The truth is that Doherty, as talented and gifted a musician as he is, probably needs more than just a simple admission to rehab. His condition goes way beyond a simple addiction to drink and drugs – when the causes of that addiction are addressed, and why he feels the need to resort to such temptation, then he might have a chance of being saved from himself.

The media coverage of stars in rehab has increased over the past two years, so much so it all adds fuel to their PR profile. That old adage that any publicity is good publicity often seems to ring true – it certainly didn't do Kate Moss any harm. There is a definite shift in the way that drug-taking is perceived by both the media and the public. Actor Robert Downey Jr served a prison sentence for cocaine abuse, and has since redeemed himself in the eyes of his public and has not stopped working since his release.

Rehab is now seen as an integral part of fame. You have to attend rehab to be seen as a true troubled celeb. Mel Gibson's booze-fuelled rant against Jews won't seriously damage his career long term, despite the significant number of influential Jewish producers, writers, agents and backers in Hollywood. Neither will Keane singer Tom Chaplin, who admitted drug abuse, have damaged record sales for the band – in fact, quite the opposite is probably true.

So even if you don't have an addiction, paranoia, anti-social behaviour or a death wish, get yourself checked in anyway, and hopefully the experts will find something that you need to be cured of. And you'll be guaranteed a bit of street cred as well.

THE DOWNSIDE OF BEING FAMOUS

You can say goodbye to privacy

You can't go to a restaurant without being stared at

You can't go out on your own in case you are stalked

You can't get drunk in nightclubs because you will be photographed

You have to give to charity otherwise you will be seen as mean

You can't go on the beach in a bikini if you have stretch marks, cellulite or a massive bum

You must be careful what you look at on your laptop, and whether there's CCTV around

You can't use your American Express Platinum cards in parking meters

You must wear plenty of makeup when you put the rubbish out

And smile when you lose an award to a sour-faced bitch of a rival

And sign thousands of autographs for sad losers who have no life

You must talk to people in comas whose parents claim they're your biggest fan

And appear on trash TV like *Love Island* to keep you in the public eye

IS IT JUST ME OR HAS EVERYONE BEEN IN REHAB?

Michael Barrymore

Peter Doherty

Tom Chaplin

Kate Moss

The Osbourne family

Kerry Katona

Sophie Anderton

Paul Gascoigne

Sadie Frost

Mel Gibson

Tony Adams

Robbie Williams

Keith Richards

Matthew Perry

Rob Lowe

Robert Downey Jr

Michael Douglas

Paul Merton

Caroline Aherne

Elton John

Robin Williams

Whitney Houston

Mike Tyson

16
Celebrity Stalkers

Another celebrity must-have – but would you be able to cope?

One high-profile celebrity agent has declared, 'Nobody is famous until they get stalked.'
So at what point does an ardent fan turn into a dangerous stalker? Well, one possible indication is when they start requesting samples of their idol's bodily fluids rather than signed photos.

Stalking is now an ever-increasing phenomenon. There is even a website called 'Gawker Stalker' that has first-person accounts of celebrity sightings, complete with the where and the when, alongside an interactive Google map. Paris Hilton, for example, was spotted sitting in a bar in Miami in a dress and sunglasses with her pet dog, and she was given 4 out of 5 for approachability. Thank God for that spotter – life would have been so much more mundane had we never known that.

It's easy to assume that your favourite celebrity lives a happy picture-perfect life, but this could not be further from the truth. Celebs live a much more hectic and stressful life than their glamorous smiles would lead us to believe – some have been repeatedly harassed, abused and even murdered by obsessed fans.

Everyone has their favourite actor, actress or singer – but there are always fans willing to take their love for their idol a step further into obsession. They cling to their pin-ups like leeches. The stalkers know everything there is to know, including where celebrities live, favourite hangouts, daily routines what toothpaste they use…and that's just the beginning. If you wanna be famous, listen up.

THE STALKEES

Meg Ryan got a restraining order against a man who claimed to be her 'husband'.

A crazed Britney Spears fan was found camping out in her garage and, although no charges were pressed, he was sent to an LA hospital for psychiatric evaluation.

A Los Angeles judge issued a restraining order against Christopher Richard Hahn, requiring him to stay at least 150 yards away from Steven Spielberg. In 1998, Jonathan Normal (who needs to change his name) was convicted of 'felony stalking' and hatching a sick plan to rape the director and hold his family hostage.

Hollywood actor Harvey Keitel was plagued by a particularly bizarre stalker who used to leave gifts for him on his doorstep. At first they were pretty innocent – fluffy rabbits, apple pies, that sort of thing. Then, one morning, he opened the front door to find she'd left a Coke bottle full of her own urine on the doorstep. Keitel, famed for his portrayals of bent cops and sleazy low-lifes, said, 'This went on for five straight days, then it seemed to stop. But the sixth day, I went to my fridge, get out a bottle of apple juice and take a swig, only to find it's urine! The crazy bitch must have broken in during the night and left it!'

So how can celebs protect themselves from these disturbed fans? While many stars have tried the traditional legal avenues of court injunctions and restraining orders, others have decided to take matters into their own hands to combat their stalkers. Keitel, for instance, played a game of tit for tat with his obsessive fan. 'I tracked the bitch down, broke into her house and crapped all over her bed – the stench was incredible and there were flies everywhere. I've not heard from her since.'

Actor Sean Penn also decided to turn the tables on a stalker who had persistently invaded his privacy by photographing and filming him in his own home through the use of high-powered telephoto lenses. Penn decided to mount a counter-surveillance operation against his tormentor. He succeeded in snatching photos of the stalker naked in the shower, masturbating in bed and sitting on the toilet, and subsequently had the pictures blown up and posted on billboards across California. That seemed to work, too!

Another star to be victimised by an obsessive fan was Julia Roberts. 'This guy, he seemed harmless enough at first, just asking for signed photos and stuff,' she recalls. 'Then he started hanging around my house and going through my trash – I had to call the cops, it was just so creepy!' When police searched the fan's apartment, they discovered a life-size effigy of Roberts fashioned from her used tampons in his bed.

Experts suggest that the typical stalker is usually a white male, in his late teens to early 40s, who may never have had a close personal relationship. Oh really? Most are withdrawn, lonely and addicted to their TV sets and *Heat* magazine. So watch out.

BJÖRK

Björk discovered some of the negative effects of fame in 1996 when a 21-year-old obsessed fan mailed an acid bomb to her home in London, and then committed suicide. The bomb, which was designed to emit sulphuric acid upon opening, was intercepted at a London post office. The impact of the incident resulted in Björk (not surprisingly) leaving England and recording her next LP in Spain.

But Björk continued to attract the most obsessed fans in the music industry, and was feeling the need to stop making music because of a stalker breaking into her mum's house and leaving threatening messages in 1998. Björk told the newspaper, *Expression*, 'This is worse than the mail bomb...that the people I love are subjected to threats because of me is horrible...and the thought alone that someone could hurt my son makes me feel sick...I feel very guilty...maybe I have to stop releasing my music...' Maybe we have a lot to be grateful to those stalkers for.

JOHN LENNON

On 8 December 1980, former Beatle John Lennon was shot down with five hollow-tip bullets as he left his apartment building in New York City. His assassin was Mark David Chapman, to whom he had just given an autograph.

Chapman would influence scores of future stalkers, and has been quoted as saying, 'I was making a statement...I became the Catcher in the Rye...Lennon became my new identity.' He became a famous person, literally overnight. He will soon be up for parole. Ironically, he could very well end up being stalked himself.

SHERYL CROW

It's not always easy to prove your stalker is dangerous. Ambrose Kappos – the alleged stalker of singer Sheryl Crow – was acquitted by a New York State jury. Kappos was charged with having stalked Crow when, in 2003, he confronted her backstage at a New York performance, where she was about to sing. He had also previously paid a visit to Crow's father, and made calls to her younger sister, in 2002, asking to meet Crow.

She was spirited into her limousine, but Kappos then ran up to it and cried, 'I am Ambrose!' Kappos claims he was 'courting' Crow and meant her no harm. But she testified she found his visit 'eerie' and it made her 'alarmed' and 'nervous'.

Being famous will always have its downside. If you achieve maximum column inches or photo shoots, you're putting your mark on society by just being a celebrity. And when that happens, society will feel they own a bit of you, and some nutters will try to make you pay. So beware…and always carry a small cattle prod and a can of Mace just in case.

17
So You Wanna Be Famous?

*'I stopped believing in Santa Claus
when my mother took me to see him in a department store,
and he asked for my autograph.'*
SHIRLEY TEMPLE

Fame is the new religion, and celebrity is god. In 2003, *New Scientist* magazine reported that one-third of Americans were suffering from something called 'celebrity-worship syndrome' (CWS). The mag said the proportion of the population affected by CWS seemed to be rising steadily....which is hardly surprising.

But why are we drawn to celebrities in the first place? It certainly seems that most people in the Western world believe they are on first-name terms with Brad, Jen, Britney or Madge. On screen, they play out our collective dreams about love, hate, good and evil. Off screen, they do it even better. But why the fascination? Why do we care about the personal lives of people we've never met?

The experts agree that the reasons are complex, but some issues seem to recur. One is that we're bored, and living through movie stars is a way of alleviating that boredom.

Another is that we're searching for identity, and fantasy relationships are becoming easier to form than real ones. That's all very well but…bollocks! Some of us just want to be famous and rich…end of!

But if you do want to be famous, first decide what you want to be famous for. You must have something going for you. What was Chantelle's appeal? Many believe it was the fact that she came over as an immature, ignorant Essex girl. No doubt about it, she seemed genuinely naïve. This is Jade Goody-land. What is not in doubt is how much she craved fame – and to achieve that through *Celebrity Big Brother* was inspired…and lucky.

She was prepared to give up everything to become a celebrity – including living in Essex. By giving up normality, she entered that rarified world of celebrity. Every single thing she says or does will be reported and analysed by the media. She has kissed anonymity goodbye, and married Preston.

You must be prepared to give up your old world. You can't get pissed without being pictured falling out of a nightclub with your pants showing (assuming you're wearing any). Your friends will tell all about your drug addictions. Your former lovers will come out of the closet and tell the press you were lousy in bed. And your bin man will get £50 for finding empty Asti Spumanti bottles/used johnnies/Botox needles in your wheelie bin. And this is just the beginning.

So what do you want to be famous for? Nowadays, it's not just pop stars and actors who are famous. You can find fame by being a gangster, a porn star, an actor, model, boxer, dancer, politician, vet, chef or a footballer. Or you can just be yourself and apply to appear on *Big Brother*, *The X Factor*, *Wife Swap* or *The Apprentice*. But if you are serious about making it, then you'd better be prepared to listen to some sound advice. Whatever you want to be, there are going to be some people you will need to impress along the way. And if the thought of being in the same room as them doesn't put you off, nothing will. The list of fame-makers includes: Simon Cowell, Max Clifford, Simon Fuller, Louis Walsh, Pete Waterman, Arlene Philips (choreographer) and Sarah Dukakis (Founder of Models 1). And if you were to impress all of them simultaneously, you'd be guaranteed a Beckham-style career, private jets, several houses around the world, your own Caribbean island…but it's never going to happen, is it?

18
Take It from the Man – Celebrity Tips from Simon Cowell

SIMON COWELL SAYS:

Believe it or not, I'm often approached by young singers who ask me what they need to do to break into the music biz. I always start by giving people the same piece of advice – don't bother. Sometimes they laugh; sometimes they shift uncomfortably. But I'm dead serious. In most cases, 'Don't bother' is the wise choice. The odds against succeeding are astronomical; in some ways, you would have better luck if you set your heart on being prime minister or becoming an astronaut.

But plenty of young singers don't listen to me when I tell them to stay on the checkout at Tesco's. They have drive and ambition and are convinced of their own talent. Good for them. They have already passed the first test, which is to make sure that they have the stomach and staying power for the music business.

You may have heard me ask contestants at auditions on *The X Factor,* 'Why are you here?' and they usually say something like, 'Because I believe I have the X factor.' Normally, the next thing you hear is the sound of a cat being strangled – and that's if you're lucky – and I start to laugh.

The truth is, not many people can really sing *and* have those extra qualities that make them a star. You will have seen me say 'no' to some people who clearly have a voice, but don't have anything different or special that will give them that star quality. I'm just saving them from a life of misery. If I put them through, they still wouldn't win the competition.

Massive stars (Meatloaf is one, for obvious reasons) don't just appear out of thin air – although sometimes it may appear as if they do – but that's just good marketing skills. The truth is, they normally emerge from somewhere else within the entertainment industry.

One way to establish yourself and to create a platform is to join a band. This can be a bitter pill for may wannabe stars to swallow, as most have huge egos. But take it from me, it's almost impossible to launch an unknown into a bona fide solo career. That's one reason shows like *The X Factor* were born. But don't just take it from me – there's a whole list of solo stars who started off in bands, and they've all done pretty well since then:

Lionel Richie (The Commodores)
Ricky Martin (Menudo)
Robbie Williams (Take That)
Bobby Brown (New Edition)
Phil Collins (Genesis)
Justin Timberlake (N'Sync)
Beyoncé Knowles (Destiny's Child)
Ronan Keating (Boyzone)
Diana Ross (Supremes)
George Michael (Wham!)
Annie Lennox (Eurythmics)

In fact, you can count the number of pop superstars who emerged fully formed as a solo artist on one hand. Nowadays, you have to take the Internet into account, and download sales are a factor now that has never existed before. Stars can be made from download sales and word of mouth, and this is a brilliant new trend of the industry.

But my advice is – if you have the chance to get noticed and to learn your trade by being a part of a band, then do it. In the same way, if you have a chance to get on television, then grab it; it's all part of how you build an audience. Look at how Kylie made it; she was already a huge star in the TV soap *Neighbours.*

Whatever you do, you are going to need someone to fight for you and champion your cause. You need representation. Managers make things happen because they have track records and contacts. Do your research because it's no good going to somebody who looks after rock bands if you want to be a pop star. The Internet is a good place to start. Managers like Louis Walsh are more likely to take your call than the head of Sony BMG.

Once you decide to devote yourself to a pop career, you're going to spend much of your time in audition rooms. As *The X Factor* and *American Idol* prove, audition rooms are where entertainment careers are born, or where they die a premature death. So it is vital to know how to handle yourself at an audition. How many times have you seen someone on *The X Factor* forget the lyrics or choose what is clearly a song that does not suit them? In my experience in the business, I believe that if you are good, you are good, and that will come across. If you're crap, you're crap. Here are my top ten tips for auditions:

- Don't copy another performer. 90 per cent of the people who come to our auditions have perfected the art of mimicry. Don't copy...I'm looking for someone who is original.

- Don't over-style yourself. Don't overdress, be yourself. I immediately hate anybody who comes in wearing sunglasses or leather trousers or weird hats. Don't.

- Don't sing and dance at the same time. It smacks of cabaret.

- Make eye contact when you sing. This is a sign of confidence. If you look at the ceiling or the floor you will appear nervous and unsure of yourself.

- Choose the right thing for your personality. A 16-year-old girl singing Patsy Cline doesn't work.

- Don't grovel when you come in − it smacks of desperation. Don't talk − sing.

- Believe in yourself the second you leave the house. People like Will Young believed in themselves the moment they woke up in the morning. Don't leave it until you're sitting in the waiting area.

- Be sure to eat and drink (not vodka) before an audition. Food is fuel and you don't want to run out of energy. Often when people forget the words of a song, I ask them, 'When did you last eat?' and they say, 'Twenty-four hours ago.' They're stupid not to give themselves the best possible chance to shine.

- Rehearse, rehearse and rehearse.

- Listen, sometimes a judge or a talent exec will see something in you but will want you to try something slightly different. Be receptive to suggestions and don't sulk.

Being a recording artist selling millions of records is probably the best job anyone could hope to have. We all know the business is ruthless and unpredictable, but the rewards are huge. The upside is, it could be you.

SIMON'S TOP FIVE FAVOURITE VOCALISTS

Frank Sinatra
Bobby Hatfield (Righteous Brothers)
Bobby Darin
Tony Bennett
Ella Fitzgerald

19
How to Get into the Tabloids

'If you want to be famous, you will be.
So when you are, come and see me.'
MAX CLIFFORD

So there you are – Max's door in Bond Street is open to you. But before you step inside, make sure you've got the clout – and the finances – to buy his time and expertise. If you want to hire Max as a your publicist when you are famous, it will cost you £15,000–£20,000 a month, so you will need to have made it big before you pick up the phone. Max was the first person that Chantelle went to see the moment she won *Celebrity Big Brother*.

'For every story I break, there are ten I stop,' says Max. 'One example was *The X Factor* winner Shayne Ward. He was recently turned over for his various relationships. During the months before that came out, his manager came to me and I stopped several other stories. When you become famous, everybody wants to talk about you – particularly your old flames.'

If you can afford Max's services, it is best to approach him before you make the big time. Simon Cowell knew that the moment he went on TV there would be trouble, and went to see Max to get his advice.

'Simon came to see me just before he appeared on *Pop Idol*. He told me that as a single bloke he had his fair share of girls, and some of them would be out for revenge. He was right. After the first *Pop Idol* show was aired, I received a number of phone calls from ex's wanting to make money out of their "relationships" with him. Simon was bright enough to know this would happen and I was able to "control" the level of publicity,' said Max.

According to Simon, going to see Max was the best investment he ever made. 'At the time, I was 41 years old and had 25 years of relationships behind me. I just knew that a few would come out of the woodwork. I nearly fell out of my chair when he told me how much he charged – but he is worth every penny. Max also became a good friend. He would be the first person I spoke to after a show – to get his opinion. He is honest, open and even ruder than me.'

Max admits that he will sometimes lie to protect people. He claims to offer a service to shield celebrities from the baying media pack on the scent of scandal. Someone about to be outed as gay or lesbian may come to him for help; he sets them up on a date with someone of the opposite sex, tips off showbiz reporters and sends them to dinner somewhere public. He says he has done this for three American stars and one British actor. So remember that on your way up.

If you cannot afford to hire Max Clifford, you can always have a go at creating your own PR. Many contestants on *Big Brother*, for example, think that they can generate column inches just by getting their tits out on television. Well, you can. Despite, or perhaps because of, that old adage that 'there's no such thing as bad publicity', people continue to underestimate the power of bad publicity. Janet Jackson did 'Nipplegate'; Liz Hurley wore 'that dress' to the *Four Weddings and a Funeral* première; Sienna Miller went out with Jude Law and Chantelle married Preston...all of which added up to acres of column inches in the tabloids and the gossip mags.

Big Brother contestants Pete Burns, Kinga and Shahbaz all made the tabloids during their five minutes of fame. But the art of publicity is to keep it going. You have to keep finding ways of reinventing yourself. Just look at Jordan and Jade Goody.

But be careful not to be the subject of a PR disaster. Prince Harry should take heed; everyone calls his Nazi-uniform-and-swastika-armband gaffe a PR disaster, but it is inconceivable that he was actually advised to turn up looking like an inept member of the Hitler Youth. It was just a case of a rather silly lad making a stupid mistake – and there's little chance of him losing his royal status because of it.

20
Celebrities on the Cover

Celebrity magazines are big business; the fame epidemic seemingly has no bounds. Almost every week, a new title hits the newsstands. In the UK, *Heat* magazine is the celebrity watchers' bible and sells over a million copies a week. And every celebrity wants to be on the cover.

Heat loves celebs, but doesn't put them on a pedestal, according to their editor Mark Frith. 'We love them even more when they wear awful dresses to the Oscars or fall over drunk outside the Met Bar. It's our sense of humour that makes *Heat* unique.

'We don't have favourites – we are led by the tabloid newspaper agenda. One week it can be George Michael – the next it's George Clooney. If celebs make news, we are interested in them because our readers are.

There is no country in the world that has the amount of tabloid newspapers we do. Tabloid newspapers can create a celebrity overnight, which is what happened with Liz Hurley. On the Monday, she wears "that" dress to a film première and by the end of the week she is the most famous person in the country. That could not happen anywhere else except Britain.

'Jade Goody sells more copies of *Heat* magazine than any one celebrity. If we put Nicole Kidman on the cover you would think, as a worldwide film star, she would sell millions of copies. She doesn't and I will tell you why – Nicole will talk about her latest film and how wonderful it was to work with her co-star, whereas Jade will tell you everything. What's going on with her love life, her work, her mum and what colour her pants are – and that's the difference. Our readers want to know every detail. People can relate to Jade but they cannot relate to an actress who just talks about her films.'

Jordan is another interesting case. Initially, she only appealed to men – so women were just not interested in reading about her. She was just someone their boyfriend fancied. Then she appeared on *I'm a Celebrity, Get Me Out of Here!* and suddenly people saw a warmer side to her when she fell in love with Peter Andre. Suddenly, she was a girl's girl. Victoria Beckham and Kate Moss remain firm favourites with readers – but that's a lot to do with fashion – and who's wearing what to where.

So what about the blokes? Love him or loathe him, putting Tom Cruise on the cover still sells mags. So, too, Brad Pitt and Johnny Depp. In the US, magazines tend to use the big film star names, while in Britain TV celebs like Ant and Dec, Simon Cowell and Russell Brand are all regularly featured.

The larger-than-life *Big Brother* contestants continue to appeal to readers of magazines like *Heat*. They may not always be on the front page of the tabloids, but if they help shift bucketloads of magazines it will help extend their 15 minutes of fame. As for Nicole Kidman – if she starts to tell us what she's eaten for breakfast, or what colour her pants are, then maybe she'll be seen on a few more covers.

HEAT MAGAZINE TOP FIVE COVER STARS 2006

Jade Goody
Kerry Katona
Jordan
Victoria Beckham
Kate Moss

US TOP FIVE COVER STARS 2006

Brad Pitt
Johnny Depp
Angelina Jolie
Tom Cruise
Jennifer Aniston

TOP-SELLING UK CELEBRITY MAGS

OK!
Closer
Heat
Hello!
Now
Reveal
Star
Sneak

21
The Power of the Internet

While an army of pub singers and wannabe Shayne Wards wait for Simon Cowell to decide if they're going to make it as pop fodder, there's a whole other gang of kids who are convinced MySpace will allow them to break free from anonymity. Somehow the MySpace idea has managed to keep its cool, although most of the wannabes posting their tracks are as deluded as the shrieking and stuttering non-starters parading across the screen in *The X Factor*.

Imagine planning and executing world domination from the comfort of your own bedroom! And if there really are little green men out there somewhere, they'll probably not bother to actually invade and waste energy using their laser beams to wipe out the human race, they'll probably just tap into the Internet, brainwash us all, and get us to commit mass suicide. The Internet is a massively powerful tool, and underestimate it at your peril.

You can use it to publicise yourself, build hype, get feedback and send your message across continents in minutes. Even now, there are prototype celebrities frantically tapping away at their keyboards, and tomorrow they could be embarking on the greatest adventure of their lives as newly discovered talent.

Remember the film *The Blair Witch Project*? Hyped online when the idea was still in its infancy, the 'documentary' horror movie was filmed with a $35,000 budget and went on to gross a staggering $248 million at the box office. If an idea takes off, then it *really* takes off.

The following performers have achieved both critical acclaim and widespread recognition from getting creative in the privacy of their own cyberspace:

THE ARCTIC MONKEYS

The first MySpace phenomenon. An amateur photographer videoed some of the band's gigs and put them on a website. They started to attract huge amounts of hits, and interest in the band grew. BBC Radio One then got wind of them.

At the 2005 Reading and Leeds Festival, the huge crowd was singing along with their material that was only available online. That year, they sold out London's Astoria, despite not being signed to a label. The band has described their rise to fame via the Internet as 'amazing'.

Highlights: Winning the Mercury Music Prize 2006, the ultimate industry award with real credibility.

Biggest Achievements: First two singles 'I Bet You Look Good on the Dancefloor' and 'When the Sun Goes Down' went straight in at Number One, and their début album *Whatever People Say I am, That's What I'm Not* holds the record for the largest amount of first week sales in UK album history. Won Best New Act 2006 Brit awards; NME awards for Best New Band and Best British Band (the only group ever to win both in the same year).

SANDIE THOM

Her 'tour', 21 Nights from Tooting, consisted of a three-week series of gigs from her basement flat in South London broadcast on the Internet. Tickets were sold but the venue only had room for six people. But the real audience were sitting in front of their PC screens all around the world. The details of the gig were posted on MySpace and people began to take notice. The first-night audience peaked at around 70,000. Her song was playlisted by Capital Virgin and BBC Radio Two.

Highlights: Playing to 70,000 people via a webcam with viewers from Russia, United States and Pakistan.

Biggest Achievement: Knocking Gnarls Barclay off Number One in 2006 with her début rereleased single 'I Wish I Was a Punk Rocker'.

LILY ALLEN

Lily went against her label Regal's wishes and uploaded demo tracks to her MySpace site. More people discovered her site and links were sent across the country. News eventually reached *NME* and online music blog *Popjustice*, both giving the demos rave reviews. BBC Radio One DJ Jo Whiley played the demo track 'LDN' on her mid-morning radio show and the industry started to buzz about Allen. Her record label brought her début single release date forward and the world opened its ears to a new, infectious, pseudo-ska brand of pop.

Highlights: Being one of the most outspoken and cocky new artists of the 21st century; calling Bob Geldof 'a cunt'; and saying she'll celebrate her success with cocaine – she later apologised and said it was irresponsible of her to say that.

Biggest Achievement: Second single 'Smile' reached Number One for two weeks in the UK with her début album *Alright, Still* charting at Number Two.

DANIEL BEDINGFIELD

Daniel holds a world record with his singing sister, Natasha Bedingfield, for being the only brother and sister to have solo number ones in UK chart history.

Highlights: After a song called 'Gotta Get Thru This', which he recorded in his bedroom, gathered momentum through the underground garage music scene, it went on to become a Number One hit in the UK in December 2001.

Biggest Achievement: Three Number One singles in the UK – 'Gotta Get Thru This'; 'If You're Not the One'; 'Never Gonna Leave Your Side'. Three further Top Ten hits and a début album *Gotta Get Thru This* that reached Number Two selling three million copies.

NIZLOPI

Folk became fab in 2005 as everyone sang about Luke and his dad in a great big digger!

Highlights: The originally released 'JCB song' charted at 160 in June 2005, but with successful Internet hype and plays on local radio and BBC Radio Two, it charted much higher on its second outing.

Biggest Achievement: Outselling Westlife 2-1 to reach Number One in December 2005 with their rereleased début single 'The JCB Song'.

GNARLS BARCLAY

They were first noticed as a backing track for a BBC Radio One advert, promoting Zane Lowe's show. Everyone started talking about it and wanted a copy, but they couldn't get one. The track was eventually released on vinyl and as a download a week ahead of its

CD single release. It went on to become record of the week on Ken Bruce's BBC Radio Two show and also on Radio One by Scott Mills, Jo Whiley, Sara Cox and DJ Spoony.

Highlights: It is the first single to top the charts consecutively for nine weeks since 1994, when Wet Wet Wet's version of 'Love Is All Around' hung around like a bad smell! It is also the longest single to top the download charts at 11 weeks.

Biggest Achievement: 'Crazy' is the only single ever in UK history to chart at Number One based on download sales alone. Gnarls had the song deleted after its ninth week at the top so people wouldn't get sick of it.

22
Where to Go and Where to Be Seen

If you like your drinks with a shot of celebrity, then you need to go to particular hangouts. Being photographed with a celeb is the quickest way of becoming one.

The latest fabulous hot spot is always changing, but there a few timeless classics in all major cities. Think the 'little black dress' of bars and clubs – they never go out of fashion.

How to get into the hot spots…that's when you need to look and act as though you're a 'somebody'. If you dress like a nobody, nobody will notice you. Lose the bad hair and the bad teeth – you need to look, think and act fabulous to become a *fabulosa*. Unless you're Shane McGowan, of course. He'd never be stopped going into or out of fashionable nightspots, as everyone's too scared they might catch something off him.

If possible, it's worth hiring a limo for the night. That way, if you don't get to become an instant celebrity, at least you've got a better chance of pulling and impressing your one-night stand.

It pays to be polite – get friendly with the doorman, the drivers parked outside, and smile charmingly at the autograph hunters, because they'll know who's in there.

Timing is important – turn up when there's an opening, a charity event or a bit of a feeding frenzy outside a hot spot. You may get papped, and you may even just slip in on someone else's coat-tails. The golden rule is: if you act like a celeb, then people will probably treat you like one.

LONDON'S HOTTEST HOT SPOTS

The Met Bar, Park Lane: This celebrity bar has been the scene of a few drunken brawls, such as the bust-up between Sadie Frost and former *Hollyoaks* actress Davinia Taylor. Past and present patrons include Mis-Teeq, Kate Moss, Liam Gallagher, P Diddy and Jennifer Lopez. The bar is also home to the Michelin-starred Nobu restaurant, a firm favourite with the crème de la crème of celebsville and WAGS (wives and girlfriends).

The Ivy, Covent Garden: Probably the most famous restaurant in the UK, The Ivy is pure celebrity heaven – most nights, you're guaranteed to see someone famous. It's a favourite with everyone from Madonna, Tom Cruise and Elton John to the Beckhams, Gordon Ramsey, Babs Windsor and Nigella Lawson.

Café de Paris, W1: Basement nightclub that also doubles as a glamorous restaurant. Recent punters include Mick Jagger, George Michael, Ronan Keating, Robbie Williams and Martine McCutcheon.

Joe Allen's, Covent Garden: Bar and regular haunt of actors and musicians like Rod Stewart.

Soho House, Soho: Private members' bar for the fabulous. Both Kylie and Robbie have been spotted here.

Groucho Club, Soho: If you can't get in, then loiter outside as you're bound to see a celeb wander past. Patrons tends to be more arty-farty than A-list.

 *The Purple Turtle, Camden*: You may have to snog some Indie muso types to get in the press, so follow in the footsteps of Kelly Osbourne and Peaches Geldof and snag yourself a skinny rocker.

The Lock Tavern, NW1: Some of the coolest celebs have moved away from the obvious hangouts. No expensive membership here and you may see some of the trendy

Notting Hill Set. Indie music, skinny jeans and continental beer. Recent spottings include groovy thesps Rhys Ifans and Samantha Morton.

Pangea, Mayfair: Princes William and Harry frequent this exclusive bar and nightclub.

Other must-go celebrity hot spots are Bond Street for spotting celebs flexing their plastic; Knightsbridge, the Harrod's end; Notting Hill; the King's Road; and, in fact, anywhere there's a fabulous department store. Harvey Nicks and Selfridges are good bets, although Top Shop in Oxford Street is a good WAG spotting venue and *you* can afford to splash some cash there, too. So shop while you spot!

NEW YORK'S NEATEST NIGHTSPOTS

Bungalow 8, West Chelsea: Any superstar, socialite and model who is worth their weight in lettuce leaves will go to this five-star lounge. You'll need five-star spending power, though, to hang out in here for any longer than five minutes.

Tao, Mid-town: This place packs them in. Regulars include Jay-Z and Beyoncé, Tom Cruise, P Diddy and some high-profile Yankees players.

Marquee: High chance of getting in and spotting Jessica Simpson, Mariah Carey and Mickey Rourke – and if you happen to be a vaguely attractive 22-year-old blonde, remember…he's always on the pull!

Koi: New York branch of the LA eatery. Fill your face alongside Leonardo Di Caprio, Mark Wahlberg and Giselle.

Butter: If you're 'It' you need to go. All the socialites plant their size zero buttocks here – Paris, Lindsay Lohan and Nicole Richie. And try to be as fussy as possible about the food – a good tip is ordering a club sandwich and saying, '…Oh, if you wouldn't mind, I'd like it on wholewheat, GM-free, organic batch loaf…dry-cured, free-range bacon from pigs who really enjoyed their lives…a micro-thin layer of extra-light mayo…breast meat from a chicken that's been left to forage on non-fertilised seed on the southern slopes of a farm in Virginia and slaughtered by a vegan farmer who has named all his animals individually…and hold the butter, please. And a Coke.'

LA'S LIKELIEST LOCATIONS

Montmartre Lounge/Nightclub, Hollywood Blvd: Where every fabulous party is held and it has the tightest velvet rope in Hollywood. Paris and Leonardo have been spotted partying here.

Runyon Canyon Park: Get a pooch and take it for a walk. Beautiful views and, most importantly, you could spot Cameron Diaz, Justin Timberlake or Drew Barrymore, all of whom enjoy a city hike. At least with a dog by your side you'll have an excuse to get entangled with the rich and famous, and may even get your canine mate to sniff their bottoms.

The Ivy: Just like the London version, you're almost guaranteed a celebrity most nights. J Lo, Tom Cruise, George Lucas and Steven Spielberg are regulars.

Kitson, Robertson Blvd: If you need some Swarovsky-encrusted flip-flops or your cashmere hoodie has shrunk in the wash, then go check it out. Britney, Jessica Simpson and Lindsay Lohan have all been spotted making use of their flexible friends here.

If clubbing's your thing, then check out The Viper Room, The Conga Room, The Whiskey Bar, The Roxy and The Troubador.

And while you're out having fun, and the cranberry champagne royales are slipping down nicely, keep your wits about you.

Here are some things *not* to do when you are famous:

- Video yourself having sex…particularly if you're on your own.
- Go on Hampstead Heath late at night…no one will

believe you when you say you were 'just having a stroll with a young lad in some bushes'.

- Pick up someone in a club and take them back to your hotel room...when you discard them eventually, they'll massacre all your pets and push poo through your letterbox.
- Go into a pub and tell everyone you are gay...unless you're Julian Clary.
- Say to a journalist 'this is off the record'...there *is* no 'off the record'.
- Send a friend photos of your anatomy from your mobile phone...unless you have a very good anatomy, you know you'll end up as the butt of someone's jokes on national television, and you'll have to have plastic surgery to get your dangly bits made more photogenic.

23
How to Look the Part

Whether they are out at a movie première or just out buying groceries, celebrities can be seen in some of the trendiest and most stylish outfits around. It may have something to do with those million-dollar pay-outs they receive. But who says you can't look just as fabulous on a budget?

Celebs have a bottomless bank account and an army of stylists, but with a bit of imagination, you can also achieve that star-quality look without breaking the bank. The key to looking like a million dollars is not found in a bunch of designer labels, but in how you put the whole ensemble together. Here are three tips that celebrities (or their stylists) use to create their star looks:

ACCESSORIES

The key to accessorising like a star is to go one step
further than you would normally go in adding this final
element to your wardrobe. For example, if you
normally wear one pin or brooch, wear two or three. If
you wear only 2-inch heels, then kick it up in a pair of
3-inchers. Sarah Jessica Parker can be seen regularly on
TV, and has fronted an ad campaign for GAP. Instead of
just pairing the company's jeans with a standard issue
GAP cardigan, the stylists for the shoot added a couple
of brooches, a fedora and some stilettos. Add these
accessories – all of which you can get from high street
stores for very little – and you will look like your stylist
has just touched you up. In the design sense, obviously.

MIX 'N' MATCH

Resist the urge to wear a designer from head to toe.
Celebrities mix and match their designers. Haven't
you seen Jessica Simpson in her Wal-Mart-esque
sweatsuit, holding a fabulous Marc Jacobs handbag
and wearing great shoes? Go on, behave like a real
diva, and mix some of your trashiest clothing with a
bit of designer bling. Throw on some Old Navy boot-
cut jeans, with a La Redoute top, and elegantly strut
around in your fancy Manolos (which you can find
heavily discounted on eBay). The online 'flea market'
is a great place to score high-fashion items below their
retail price, as is eBay.

MAKE IT FIT

In this 'off-the-rack-on-my-back' shopping culture, the importance of tailored clothing has been thrown away. The reason why the stars look fabulous in their clothes is because they are tailored. However, you don't have to be a billionaire in order to have your clothes tailored – just head to your local dry cleaners. A little nip and tuck in your new threads will make you look great, and will avoid you having to have a little nip and tuck elsewhere.

24
How to Become a Top Model

I n America they say, 'If you can dream, you can do it!' And there's no getting away from it – the best models have great faces and bodies, ones that we all want to aspire to, so if you've got the face of a baby rhino, and the body of a sumo wrestler, you've got your work cut out. But there is still hope.

One of the biggest reality TV successes in the US is *America's Next Top Model*. Created by supermodel Tyra Banks, who executive produces the series, the programme chronicles the transformation of everyday young gals into, well, top supermodels. Fourteen contestants live together and vie for the grand prize – an opportunity to be managed by top agency Ford Models, a fashion spread in *Elle* magazine, and a

$100,000 contract with *CoverGirl*. Now every schoolgirl wants to be a model.

Modelling has always been big business and, apart from all the garrotting that pirates did in the 17th and 18th centuries, it's probably the most cut-throat. Only a handful wannabes actually make it to the top to command the millions like Kate Moss and Gisele Bundchen. But if you have your sights set on being a glamour model, then splash on the fake tan, perk up your boobs, have a bum lift, and prepare to let it all hang out on Page Three of the *Sun*.

How many adverts have you seen in newspapers and on the Internet stating 'Do You Want to Be a Top Model? We Can Help'. The fact is, most of them are con artists preying on young people's dreams. They will ask you to pay a fee, they may take photos of you (for another fee) then 'put you on their books'. Then what? Normally nothing. So you have been warned.

Being taken on by one of the top agencies like Ford or Elite is almost unheard of – you probably have more chance of winning the lottery. But some girls – and blokes – have been, so there's always a chance. We have all heard of model 'scouts' whose job it is to scour the country, hang around in shopping centres, go to discos, or loiter outside school gates looking for the next fresh-faced, modern look. And it does happen – Kate Moss was one such 'lucky' girl. Most kids would kill to have her life, and it does appear glamorous. But if that life is possibly going to kill her in the end – through drugs, alcohol abuse or just being romantically attached to Pete Doherty – then is it really all that it's cracked up to be?

If your heart is set on being the next top model, Matti Gidilevich, an agent at Elite, one of the world's largest agencies, has some sound advice for you wannabe Kate Mosses:

- We look for all styles of models to promote through our network; editorial and commercial models. We are always looking for this year's new face. Fashion and 'the look' are forever changing. So it could be you.
- Don't have an attitude.
- Don't be late for appointments for castings.
- If you are having photos taken for your portfolio, it always helps to have very clear pictures, with great lighting, and little makeup. I often find it difficult to see what a person looks like when they use a webcam to take their pictures.
- Modelling is a business and, as a model, you are your own business! Like any business, it takes time, effort, commitment and patience to become a successful model. Success does not happen overnight.
- For models, a casting or a 'go see' is a job interview, and should be regarded as such. Time and time again, I hear from clients that models seem ill-prepared.
- Would you show up to a job interview with a potential employer wearing sneakers, with your hair not done, without a resumé? No.

- Typically in our market, we look for girls who are 5ft 8in and taller. Girls who are 5ft 10in and up, of course, are better suited for the European catwalks should they have the rest of the package (confidence, experience, and a strong portfolio).

- There are never any guarantees. We as agents know what clients want, and supply our clients with just that. It is also our job to provide management for our models. We can open the door for the models, but it's up to the individual to walk through it. It's those models that can work with clients and be engaging, polite and, most of all, professional, who are the models that are going to get booked again by that client.

TOP MODELLING AGENCIES

Elite
Storm
Models One
Ford
Select
Take Two
IMG
Next
Metropolitan

25
The Fast-track to Fame

If you are lazy and don't fancy becoming a famous pop star, model or TV star, why not throw a 'brick' at some else who is famous. If you take this literally, you could end up on the wrong end of a GBH charge. The Americans, though, use this term to describe insulting someone, and this has been a tried and tested route for many of our best-known celebrities. They've done little of worth themselves, but have spent almost all their energy disparaging others…and becoming famous for it.

Walter Winchell was the most influential American newspaper columnist of the 1930s–40s, a time when newspapers were the most powerful media in the world. His formula for success? 'The fastest way to become famous,' he said, 'is to throw a brick at someone famous.' Winchell fought publicly with entertainment's biggest names, from Al Jolson to Josephine Baker to Lucille Ball. Later in his career, he swung toward political reporting. Winchell championed an unprecedented third term for President Franklin Roosevelt as well as the Red Scare for Joe McCarthy. He threw bricks in every direction, and this made him one of the most famous men in America.

Winchell's tactics have been adopted and adapted by scores of ambitious individuals and organisations. How did Ralph Nader become famous? By attacking General Motors. How did Jesse Jackson become famous? By claiming that racism is systemic at virtually every major US corporation, then attacking those corporations one by one – Anheuser-Busch, AT&T, Viacom, Verizon, Ford and so on. Not only has this made him famous, it has made him wealthy, with an annual income estimated to exceed $300,000.

How did style guru Mr Blackwell become famous? By issuing an annual list of the Worst Dressed Women in the World, and thus attacking some of the most famous females on the planet. The former fashion designer has been casting scathing insults at the rich and famous for nearly 50 years now, and there are few who fail to quake with fear when his annual list is published. In the past he has fired rhyming critiques at:

MARIAH CAREY

'The world applauds your musical emancipation...but please, leave that body to our imagination.'

PARIS HILTON

'The Burger Queen Sensation may be very rich – but she still looks like yesterday's cheesecake... with a side of kitsch.'

ANNA NICOLE SMITH

'Queen Kong.'

SHAKIRA

'Coiffure by Medusa...clothes by the Marquis de Sade.'

LINDSAY LOHAN

'The Teen Scream defines "Fashion Fright" – looks like she's aged 30 years overnight.'

RENÉE ZELLWEGER

'Runs the gamut from Kewpi Doll Dreck to Red Carpet Wreck...she looks like a painted pumpkin – on a pogo stick.'

Note also the sudden ascent that comedian/actress Janeane Garofalo's career has taken since she took the lead in attacks on President Bush's policy in Iraq. Agree or disagree with her, there's no doubt that throwing bricks at the White House has benefited her. 'Before this, I was a moderately well-known character actress,' Garofalo recently told the *Washington Post*. 'Now, I'm almost famous.' Famous enough to warrant an ABC sitcom, as well as more than 53,000 Google hits using her name alone. Throw the right brick at the right person, and you gain fame.

Obviously, throwing a brick isn't for everyone. It takes a strong stomach, a steady nerve and the willingness to dodge a few bricks thrown back at you. But it can work, big time, if all else fails.

26
Making it Big in America

*'I'm doing a little talent show in America –
and I'm going to be the Joan Collins of pop TV.'*
SIMON COWELL

If you wanna be famous – *really* famous – go to America. When you have a hit record or a top-rating TV show in the US, big just gets bigger. TV shows like *Survivor, American Idol* and *America's Next Top Model* have millions of viewers glued to their screens every night. When you get 35 million people watching you, you really do feel that you have made it – just ask Simon Cowell.

Reality television in America is kind of hard to miss – it's everywhere and becoming increasingly hard to avoid. *Temptation Island* was featured on the cover of *People* magazine. *Big Brother* airs five days a week and could be viewed on the Internet 24 hours a day. And the *Survivor* finale dominated the front page of the *New York Post* after gaining ratings that rivalled those of the Super Bowl.

Some US TV critics have said that the popularity of shows such as *Survivor, Big Brother* and *Temptation Island* is a sign that the country has degenerated into a nation of voyeurs. Oh, come on...as humans, we've always been interested in what other humans do, think about, talk about, behave like...it's just that when we all lived in caves, it wasn't quite so easy to twitch curtains (not invented), peer through your window (not invented) and watch your neighbour trying to get off with his mate's wife. (Well, maybe that happened quite a bit.) Nowadays, we can just flick a switch, settle back with some Pringles and a Budweiser, and watch the entire spectrum of human experience in all its glory. And we don't even have to run out of our caves and hunt down a wild boar for dinner. We just get the wild bore to pop down to Tesco's and cook it for us!

The critics' major grouse is that Americans seem hooked on the programmes in which ordinary people compete in week-long contests while being filmed 24 hours a day. Some commentators moan that the shows peddle blatant voyeurism, with shameless exhibitionists as contestants. But isn't all television voyeurism to some extent? And isn't reality TV the natural extension of that? If the programme makers think that there's a market for watching people degrading themselves, then it's up to the viewer to decide whether they want to sit there for 24 hours a day, or switch off and get a life for themselves. In the land of the free, viewers have never had as much freedom as they do today.

One aspect that all reality TV shows have in common is their competitive nature. Contestants are usually pitted against one another for a cash prize, or at least for something that motivates them to win. The first *Survivor* series climaxed with one contestant, Susan Hawk, launching into a vengeful tirade against a one-time friend and ally before casting the vote that deprived her of the million-dollar prize. It makes sense, then, that fans of both *Survivor* and *Temptation Island* tend to be competitive. The truth is, Americans really enjoy that competitive element, perhaps more so than any other nation on earth, and the viewing public just can't get enough.

So if you want to sing for Simon, Paula and Randy, be hired by Donald Trump, or strut your stuff for Tyra, then you'd better head across the pond because reality television in the US is way out in front.

BRITS IN AMERICA

Historically, crossing the Atlantic can be a lesson in humility for British pop stars. For every Beatles, Coldplay and now James Blunt, there's a Keane and Robbie Williams who just don't make the cut in the US.

However, Brits specialising in put-downs, sarcasm or, in some cases, downright rudeness, are enjoying unprecedented success on US television.

The trailblazer of brutal bluntness is *The X Factor* and *American Idol* judge Simon Cowell, whose insults have become legendary in the world of reality television:

- 'I have never, ever, been in so much pain listening to somebody sing.'
- If you were a horse, after that performance, they'd shoot you.'
- 'Well, we could be forgiven for thinking we'd never heard that song before...you killed it...you totally murdered it.'
- 'OK...you're out of tune, you're out of time, and you know what...you're out of here.'
- 'Look, I know you were doing your best...thank God we didn't have to hear your worst.'

He has been followed by former *Mirror* editor Piers Morgan, now the judge on summer ratings hit *America's Got Talent*. There's also Jo Frost, whose series *Supernanny* is into its third season, and Gordon Ramsay, whose brand of short-tempered perfectionism in *Hell's Kitchen* frequently reduces contestants to tears. He told one unlucky cook, 'That looks like dehydrated camel's turd.'

Sir Ian McKellen, Ricky Gervais, John Cleese, Jude Law, Orlando Bloom, Keira Knightley...they all have very healthy profiles 'over there', but success for British pop acts still remains elusive. The last band to really make it in the US were the Spice Girls and they stopped making records eight years ago.

'British people tend to assume that pop is British...it isn't – it's American,' says John Aizlewood, a London-

based music writer and broad-
caster. 'Europe likes America's
music. It's more that America
doesn't need British music.'

Americans who embraced
Beatlemania, progressive rock
and the New Romantics
have been left cold by
Britpop. Music industry
reports say the British share
of *Billboard*'s annual Top 100
albums chart has plummeted from a high of 32 per cent
in 1986 – when bands like Duran Duran, Pet Shop
Boys and Simple Minds rode the British wave – to just
0.2 per cent.

There has long been a fertile musical cross-
pollenation across the Atlantic. Americans invented
rock 'n' roll, but Britain produced the Beatles and the
Rolling Stones. Punk may have started with the
Ramones and the New York Dolls, but the Sex Pistols
and the Clash inspired a new generation of American
punks. Now, it seems, all the traffic is in one direction

Industry figures are so worried they have urged the
government to set up a musical mission in the United
States where other countries are having far more
impact, which is slightly embarrassing and somewhat
upsetting for UK acts. Some say British acts lack the
stamina to make it in the United States. Over the last
few years, a stream of British music heroes – from Oasis

to Robbie Williams – have crossed the Atlantic and come back chastened.

Aizlewood says British bands often underestimate the sheer slog of touring required to make an impact in the United States. Others have criticised British musicians as too insular, or too inoffensive to gain an international audience in the era dominated by R&B. 'There isn't anyone who's really bright enough or original enough to make a global impact,' said Aizlewood. 'That's not the decline of British music. It's just one of those phases. Because America is so huge and so diverse, everything you want musically is available,' he added. 'That's why it's so difficult to break through.'

According to the industry report, 92 per cent of all records sold in the United States are by American artists. Paul McCartney is one of the only British rock stars who continue to ride high in the US – with his 2005 tour grossing millions. But it's unlikely that his recent work has been responsible for Sir Macca's popularity. The Beatles are still revered in the US as a phenomenon, with 'Yesterday' being confirmed as world's most popular song with over 6,000,000 airplays in the USA alone. Now *that's* what I call music!

You have only to watch *American Idol* and *The X Factor* and appreciate the differences in the song choices that contestants make at auditions to see how we remain worlds apart in musical tastes. Can you imagine Michelle McManus winning *American Idol*? According to *Forbes* magazine, Britain is running out of celebrities with global pulling power.

In 2006, there were just six Brits on the *Forbes* Celebrity 100, and that's if you count Madonna, who only pretends to be British. David Beckham's US star continues to rise, coming in at number 26, up from 56 last year. Posh will be pleased.

Two of the remaining five are ageing rockers – Elton John and Rod Stewart – who can't last for ever. Shouldn't we sound the alarm? After all, Americans expect more from the UK because the two countries share a language and large aspects of a common culture. Well, almost.

CULTURAL EXCHANGE

American celebrities have regularly travelled to the UK to gain a bit of culture, Madonna being the most recent. By the same token, British celebrities have long journeyed to New York and Los Angeles to gain a bit of cash and surround themselves with a bit of bling. Many have stayed on.

There is still some interchange, of course, but British actors, though talented as ever, are not getting the starring roles they once did. Americans have also lost their taste for British writers, at least in the best-selling fiction category, with J K Rowling being the only exception.

No one can say for sure what is causing the shortage of Brits in the top ranks of celebrity, but a few theories have emerged. One is that movies have become more low-brow than ever, with action stars dominating the box office. These stars tend to be rugged American types, not classy or bemused Englishmen like Cary Grant or Hugh Grant. They like their stars with balls of steel – think Vin Diesel and 50 Cent, rather than Stephen Fry or Daniel Day-Lewis.

Sport is another area where we cannot compete; Americans just don't get our 'quaint' national games, or the way we play them. Britain's problem in producing sports celebrities is a perennial one. We insist on playing football rather than grid iron and, worse, cricket rather than baseball. Though Americans will give a nod to a soccer star on rare occasions – provided, like David Beckham, he marries the right clothes horse, has the right face and has versatile hair – they have never tolerated cricketers and never will. Brits, quite literally, refuse to play the game.

A third cause of the British celebrity shortage is that the culture (in Britain as well as in the US) has become more focused on the Everyman who appears on so-called 'reality' television. But America has plenty of nobodies of its own and hardly needs to import nobodies from Britain. And vice versa. Either way, talent-based celebs get crowded out.

Finally, there is the Royal Family. Royals remain über-celebrities, famous by birthright. Our list rules preclude royals from being named in the Celebrity 100. But Jessica Simpson and Paris Hilton and their ilk will always have an important place in US celebrity culture. In Britain, that place is occupied by royals, sucking the air from potential celebrities lacking royal birth. The only exceptions to this rule are national heroes such as Graham Norton, Julian Clary and Dale Winton – all bona fide A-listers and honorary members of our royal celebrity family – they're self-confessed queens.

27
Is It Just Me or Is Everyone Getting Divorced?

Even if being rich and famous can be hazardous to a marriage, a high-profile split can do wonders for your celebrity stock. So if you haven't got a pre-nup, you could be in for a shock.

COLIN MONTGOMERIE
The Ryder Cup hero recently agreed to give his childhood sweetheart Eimear half of his £30 million fortune after their marriage collapsed in bitterness. Was that a 'fairway' to split up his hard-earned fortune, or should he have driven her off with a smaller bit of wedge?

NEIL DIAMOND
Neil Diamond and Marcia Murphey split in 1996 after the singer admitted his music left little time for

marriage. After paying out £88 million, his music's not quite so much of a beautiful noise.

HARRISON FORD

Harrison Ford had to pay out £68 million following his affair with *Ally McBeal* star Calista Flockhart. A bitter pill to swallow for the raider of the lost heart.

LIONEL RICHIE

Lionel Richie pays his ex-wife Diana Alexander £100,000 a month including an £8,000 clothes allowance. 'Pay you…slay me…'

TOM CRUISE

When Tom and Nicole split she got a tasty £63 million! After all, as a millionairess in her own right, she needed Tom's millions to get over the trauma of having spent 'intimate' time with the pocket-sized Scientologist.

STEVEN SPIELBERG

Steven Spielberg and Amy Irving's £58 million settlement in 1989 revealed that even the most ironclad pre-nuptial deals can be undone. But then if you do draft it on the back of a napkin….

BRUCE WILLIS

When Bruce and Demi Moore broke up in 2000 she got £52 million. The *Die Hard* star says he still loves

Demi 'with all my heart'. She says she still loves him 'with all his money'.

KEVIN COSTNER

Kevin Costner's divorce from Cindy Silva cost him £47 million. Having had to sit through *Waterworld*, she deserved every penny she got.

KENNY ROGERS

Kenny had to cough up £40 million to divorce Marianne Gordon in 1993. Luckily, he still has a tidy back catalogue to keep him going through the long, lonely winter evenings.

JAMES CAMERON

The *Titanic* director walked out on Linda Hamilton in 1999 for up-and-coming actress Suzy Amis. The settlement was £30 million, which isn't a great deal when you're part-exchanging a slightly older model. Plenty of miles still on the clock, though.

MICHAEL DOUGLAS

Michael Douglas paid his ex-wife Diandra £26 million after she claimed that he was a sex addict who cheated throughout their 18-year marriage. Plenty for Catherine to look forward to, then.

CELEBRITY WEDDING COSTS

Peter Andre & Jordan – £1.7 million
David & Victoria Beckham – £1 million
Catherine Zeta-Jones & Michael Douglas –
£1 million
Cheryl Tweedy & Ashley Cole – £1 million
Anthea Turner & Grant Bovey – £450,000
Bryan McFadden & Kerry Katona – £300,000
Joan Collins & Percy Gibson – £380,000
Liza Minelli & David Guest – £100,000
Tamzin Outhwaite & Tom Ellis – £30,000

FACES OF THE FUTURE – WHO'S HOT TO TROT?

Who will lead the next generation of hot celebs? Can anyone take Paris Hilton's tiara? Will anyone eclipse Jordan's massive...ego? Not in the near future, certainly, but there is a host of up-and-coming, hot new stars already making an impact in the tabloids. Here are a few tips for the top:

PEACHES GELDOF

Precocious, mouthy and still just a teenager. Peaches has already made inroads into party land and is a contender for Britain's answer to Paris Hilton. You can spot her all over London with her 15-year-old sister Pixie in tow.

She has style, talent (as a DJ/writer/TV presenter) and the tabloids love her. Not sure what dad can do about it.

LILY ALLEN

The *enfant terrible* has been stirring up trouble ever since she was expelled from school, doing drugs as a teenager and performing her ska/punk songs. Genuine talent, great style and a big gob could see her well into the next celebrity decade.

MARISSA MONTGOMERY

The blonde, blue-eyed, 19-year-old Chelsea girl known for designing hot lingerie called Pussy Glamore. She's the new 'posh totty' on the London scene. Ambitious, glitzy and, by all accounts, a stayer.

PETE BENNET

The 2006 *Big Brother* winner, 24 year-old Pete helped millions understand what Tourette's syndrome actually was. Following his well-publicised fling with housemate Nikki, he started writing songs with top song writer Guy Chambers and the world is waiting for him on a plate. With mass appeal and a helping hand from Max Clifford, Pete could be around much longer than his housemates.

MIQUITA OLIVER

She was just 16 when she started presenting TV's *PopWorld*. She is the niece of singer Neneh Cherry and got the job after telling Britney Spears she was 'an idiot'. She is pals with Lily Allen and has already been papped falling out of the best bar in London. Great chance to join the new celeb set.

YOU

So you think you've got it in you to make it as a celeb? Could you really be the next big thing? Have you checked your wardrobe; fixed your makeup; rehearsed, rehearsed, rehearsed; gone to the most exclusive clubs; been seen with the trendiest people; got yourself snapped by the paps; planned your audition tape; worked on your voice; had a bum lift, a nose job, liposuction, Botox, chin, lip and cheek implants; had your boobs plumped up and your varicose veins removed; behaved like a diva; married someone beautiful but dim; divorced them and been paid a fortune in settlement; snorted cocaine, injected crack, smoked weed, taken uppers, downers and siders; got smashed on Bacardi Breezers and retched in a gutter outside Stringfellow's; been caught on video in a three-in-a-bed romp with a guy, a gal and a transsexual; and had the smallness of your privates splattered across the front page of the *News of the World*?

If so...welcome to the big, shiny, happy world of celebrity, daaaaaahling!